Affirmative
Action
& the
Woman Worker

Jennie Farley

Affirmative Action & the Woman Worker

Guidelines for Personnel Management

amacom **A Division of**
American Management Associations

791105

Library of Congress Cataloging in Publication Data

Farley, Jennie.
  Affirmative action & the woman worker.

    Includes index.
    1. Women--Employment--United States. 2. Affir-
mative action programs--United States. 3. Personnel
management--United States. 4. Sex discrimination in
employment--United States. I. Title.
HD6095.F35   658.3   78-11719
ISBN 0-8144-5498-4

First Printing

Preface

THIS book is an analysis of the impact of equal opportunity legislation on certain personnel practices affecting women in American work organizations. The book has limited aims. It is not a legal treatise on the details of the laws known best to attorneys (for whom, some say, the legislation already serves as a full employment act). Nor is it a consideration of all aspects of personnel management, although it can be argued that the field as a whole is undergoing the biggest change since the Industrial Revolution. It is not a discussion of whether affirmative action programs represent a contradiction of American ideals or an extension of them. While philosophers debate that, personnel managers have the immediate problem of trying to obey laws that already bind them. Philosopher John Rawls holds that the most nearly just system is designed by people who do not know where they will be in it. This is a home truth for personnel practitioners, who know full well that policies they champion and implement affect no one so much as they themselves in their daily work.

Finally, this work is not a theoretical discussion of why women are where they are in the social order of the twentieth century. Valuable feminist analysis is being developed by scholars of both sexes in many disciplines, including history, the classics, anthropology, political science, biology, and literature. My training is in sociology; my interest, in the practical and the applied. In this book I have tried to analyze changes in personnel policy and practice by sharing with the reader the experiences that personnel managers have shared with me and the results of social science research that seem pertinent to the day-to-day problems in implementing affirmative action.

Today, some personnel practitioners find themselves bewildered as to how they can do three things at once: (1) serve the best interests of management, as they are paid to do; (2) act in good faith in complying with confusing and sometimes contradictory laws commanding them to take affirmative action with respect to certain classes of workers and prospective employees; and (3) still protect the rights of all men as well as women, all members of majority groups as well as minorities.

Proper motivation, once thought to be a sound defense even if it resulted in an improper action, no longer serves to protect an industrial organization from a charge of discrimination. The Equal Employment Opportunity Commission has spelled that out clearly in its guidebook *Affirmative Action and Equal Employment:* "It is the *consequences* of employment practices, *not* the *intent*, which determines whether discrimination requiring remedial action exists." Furthermore, if a survey should show that minorities and women are not participating in an organization *"at all levels in reasonable relation to their presence in the population and the labor force, the burden of proof is on . . . [the employer] to show that this is not the result of discrimination, however inadvertent."*

The purpose of this book is to consider the nature of the personnel manager's responsibility toward women workers. Chapter 1 examines the situation that has prompted passage of the laws. Why have legislators seen fit to intervene in areas where employers were once left to their own devices?

What is the nature of this far-reaching legislation, and to what extent has it helped the woman worker? Chapter 2 reviews the development of the personnel function and the role women have played in it in industrial organizations.
Chapters 3, 4, and 5 are devoted to an analysis of three aspects of personnel practice: recruitment, selection, and training. To be sure, a great many other personnel activities could have been chosen: wage and salary administration; the conduct of collective bargaining; the administration of benefits, especially those linked with retirement. But these aspects of the personnel function have not been affected by the EEO laws so directly and so profoundly as have the tasks involved in finding new workers, choosing among them, and training them to make the best possible contribution to the organization.

Chapter 6 is devoted to a consideration of the minority woman worker and her extraordinary status as a member of two protected classes. Chapter 7 considers the status of women in the public sector as opposed to that of women in profit centers and concludes with examples of women who are organizing for change—and bringing it about. Chapter 8 examines the female workforce by level—that is, the kinds of jobs women hold as blue collar workers, clerical employees, salesworkers, professionals, and managers. Chapter 9 is devoted to the day-to-day problems with (and for) women workers, including what they like to be called, the development of a "new etiquette," the difficulties inherent in trying to bring about attitude change, and the problem of how to build career ladders and people them prudently.

Chapter 10 examines what some consider to be the "hardest problems"—those relating to women who are not only workers but mothers, to women who differ from the majority by age as well as sex, and to women who are lesbians. The chapter also considers the problems of sexual harassment at work and suggests ways a company can protect itself and its employees, both men and women. A final section is devoted to the development of romantic relationships at work and how the personnel office should be "coping with Cupid." Chapter 11 examines how little we really know about men and women and suggests certain problems—such as expecting too much too soon from new research, new laws, and new policies and practices. Chapter 12 is devoted to a synthesis of the materials presented in earlier chapters, together with some predictions about issues that personnel managers will have to face as men and women come together as equals at work.

The equal opportunity legislation is in place to protect all of us—woman and man, white and black, worker and manager—from unjust illegal treatment. I believe it has the potential for making worklife and homelife more satisfying for us and for our daughters and sons. It is this conviction that prompted me to write about personnel management and women's work in the United States and the way each is changing in response to the new legislation. I have sat in on many educational sessions mounted by management in higher education that sought to improve communication on affirmative action between top administrators and the community. One sad reality is that the most interested parties to these meetings—and the most numerous—are women workers and prospective workers. Perhaps this is unique to higher education. But I don't think so.

Throughout the book I have illustrated certain points about personnel practices with evidence from academic life, not because colleges and universities are earning A's for compliance or because they are in the failing column, but because more research has been done on campus than elsewhere. Colleges are quite like industrial organizations in that some are good, some not so hot. Within each kind of organization, there are pockets of resistance and misogyny and havens where women workers find friends and support.

I believe that personnel has not only a legal but a moral obligation to try to see that justice is done. The new laws are making our field and our work more frustrating than ever before but, at the same time, more challenging and ultimately more influential in shaping what happens where most of us spend most of our waking hours: at work.

Acknowledgments

This book was made possible by personnel managers who shared their experiences in implementing affirmative action in their work organizations with my students and with me. I am also indebted to my colleagues Alice H. Cook, Gregory Dela Cruz, Thomas DeCotiis, Lee D. Dyer, Felician Foltman, Jennifer Gerner, Shirley Harrell, Frank B. Miller, Susan Muller, Rhoda Possen, Robert Risley, Robert Stern, William Wasmuth, and William B. Wolf for their helpful comments on portions of the manuscript.

I am also grateful to the editors at the American Management Associations for their professional guidance; to Nancy Towle Adshead, Jane Van Wagner Condon, Joan Condon Guilfoyle, Dorothy Jane Van Wagner Towle, and Howard Albert Towle for their assistance; and to Donald Thorn Farley, Claire Hamlin Farley, Anne Tiffany Farley, and Peter Towle Farley for theirs.

Jennie Farley

Contents

R
t.

[Payment] for a man, 50 silver
shekels; for a woman, 30.
—*Leviticus 27:3–7.*

1

The Nature
of the Problem

TIME was when some personnel managers could enjoy a
joke about the ideal candidate. "Send me a black female
college graduate," they'd say to one another. "Lots of
brownie points there. And even more if she's a Spanish-
surnamed handicapped lesbian veteran!" Everybody
would laugh. At a conference one personnel man began
with that little jest, which he delivered with a hearty professional chuckle. In that crowded conference room, he was
the only one laughing. Today, it is recognized that personnel problems relating to women as applicants and as workers can be aggravating, time-consuming, expensive, and
even dangerous. Casual slips can bloom into lush legal
tangles that are costly in emotion, time, and money. Whatever else these problems are, they are not funny.

In 1940 the U.S. Department of Labor was enforcing 16
statutes and executive orders affecting personnel practices,
of which comparatively few differentiated workers by sex.
By 1960 the number had grown to 40; by 1977, there were
no fewer than 130.[1] An administrator of the New York State

[1] Fred K. Foulkes and Henry K. Morgan, "Organizing and Staffing the
Personnel Function," *Harvard Business Review,* Vol. 55, No. 3 (May–June
1977), pp. 142–154, p. 148.

1

human rights law has pointed out that there are currently 225 ways an employer can violate that legislation alone. Management has to be alert to avoid illegal practices with respect to a worker's sex—the theme we shall concentrate on here. But other characteristics also provide potential for legal trouble and ethical dilemmas: age, race, creed, color, national origin, mental or physical disability, marital status, criminal record, and record of bringing complaints against other employers. This list excludes mention of "affectional preference" (heterosexual or homosexual) and status as parent and/or age of dependents. These two areas may well be covered soon. The number of federal and state directives is mushrooming; their impact on the personnel function has brought about the greatest change in management practice since the Industrial Revolution. Clearly, the biggest group of workers and potential workers affected are women, who make up 52 percent of the population of the United States and 41 percent of the citizens in the paid workforce.

The Data Base

Until recently, studies of the social organization of work often omitted consideration of the sex of the worker. Male researchers tested male-oriented theories with evidence gathered in male-dominated work settings. Laboratory studies sometimes omitted women from the sample population because (as was the case with the achievement motivation investigations) women tested so differently from men that it was difficult to generalize from the data. Other times, researchers included women in their studies but neglected to report that they did or in what proportions. It is as though millions of American women workers were invisible.

The neglect of the male/female dimension in work studies is well illustrated by the often cited Hawthorne experiments. In 1927, at the Hawthorne plant of the Western Electric Company in Chicago, a series of investigations was undertaken to test the impact of variations in lighting, rest periods, length of working day, and other factors on production. The experimenters changed the conditions under which groups of workers worked and production went up. They changed the conditions again and production still went up. They changed the conditions a third time and production went up. Finally, they reverted to the original conditions. Production continued to climb. The conclusion? A work organization is a human group, complex and difficult to understand. Workers appreciate attention. The Hawthorne experiments provided a turning point in the study of the workplace; they are cited as such in virtually every course in industrial sociology.

The official reports of these studies passed over the sex differentiation of the workers lightly. Not until 1974 did researchers go back to the evidence to ask if the sex of the workers might have made any difference. Acker and Van Houten, who reviewed all the Hawthorne data, have suggested that the fact that they were women affected their performance at work more than was realized. The women workers in the experiments were selected differently from men, treated differently, and subjected to quite different medical exams, to which they reacted quite differently.[2] It is clear that a full understanding of what happened at Hawthorne cannot be gained without taking into account that some of the work groups were comprised of women.

Similarly, in studies of leadership style little serious attention has been paid to the sex of the leaders and the sex of the followers. Only in 1974 did Bartol gather evidence to suggest that, although women leaders are different from men, they are not necessarily (as had been thought) likely to be more authoritarian. Indeed, Bartol's data suggest that women with a "high need for dominance" do not have a negative effect on reported work satisfaction of their subordinates.[3] Many researchers have noted that, until recently,

[2] Joan Acker and Donald R. Van Houten, "Differential Recruitment and Control: The Sex Structuring of Occupations," *Administrative Science Quarterly*, Vol. 19, No. 2 (June 1974), p. 152.

[3] Kathryn M. Bartol, "Male Versus Female Leaders: The Effect of Leader Need for Dominance on Follower Satisfaction," *Academy of Management Journal*, Vol. 17, No. 2 (June 1974), p. 225.

the whole field has been slanted toward men's perspectives and men's problems, with men as subjects and men as researchers. Sociologist Pamela Roby has summarized the problem neatly, showing that the "sociology of work" has been, by and large, the "Sociology of men's work." [4]

An interesting exception to the general lack of attention accorded women workers was published in 1943, during World War II.[5] It was a set of guidelines summarizing what social scientists had discovered about the nature of women, to aid supervisors in resolving women's special problems at work. Now, 35 years later, it is instructive to learn that women could do what had been thought to be men's jobs. And do them well. The publication points out that women seemed able to adjust more readily to routine jobs than men, that women needed more praise and encouragement at work, and that some problems arose because women had been more "pampered" than men. But, the guidelines continue, most of women's troubles on the job—and, by implication, the problems that come about in supervising them—arose, not from women's nature but from their lack of familiarity with machinery, customs, and expectations. The report notes that if a personnel department provided special counseling or training for women, it was sharply criticized for "coddling" them.

Today personnel managers may find that publication condescending in its references to women as "girls" and chuckle at the paragraph that alludes delicately to certain physiological problems—apparently meaning the menstrual cycle. But managers will find the issues familiar. At the very least, the publishers were thinking about the problem and seeking to summarize evidence that might suggest solutions. And their overall conclusion, that the

[4] Pamela Roby, "Sociology and Women in Working-Class Jobs," in Marcia Millman and Rosabeth Moss Kanter (eds.), *Another Voice: Feminist Perspectives on Social Life and Social Science* (Garden City, N.Y.: Doubleday/Anchor, 1975), pp. 203–239.
[5] *The Supervision of Women on Production Jobs*, Research Report 2 (New York: American Management Association, 1943).

principles of good supervision are the same whether the workers are men or women, cannot be faulted. Still, the basic texts in the field often sound as though they are all about men (*Men and Management; Man, Work, and Society; Men at Work*). They often are. The anthology *Man, Work, and Society* provides us with 612 pages on the sociology of work. But the index shows no entry under "women," "female," "sex," or even "girls." There is one entry in the index under "wives: See corporation wives." This leads the reader to a chapter on the problems male executives have with their wives. If a corporation wife is an alcoholic or too sexually demanding, the writer observes, her husband may have problems at work. The first serious treatments of the problems of women workers—and, in fact, of the curious and stressful role of corporate wives—have only now begun to appear.[6]

There is no question that researchers have neglected women workers. We know little about the way girls make career choices, about how women's work for pay affects the economy, about the occupational safety and health of women workers, or about factors affecting women's decisions to work even when their children are infants. We know even less about the job most American women do whether they work for pay outside the home or not: housewife. Our standard reference work, the *Dictionary of Occupational Titles*, lists and describes some 20,000 jobs held by Americans. Until last year, a person wanting to look up "Housewife" was directed to "See Maid, General." Briggs has found that jobs generally held by women have lower skill ratings than jobs usually held by men.[7] Those skill classifications in the *Dictionary of Occupational Titles* reflect reality: the world of work is "balkanized" into women's jobs and men's jobs. And women's skills are valued less than men's.

[6] See, for example, Rosabeth Moss Kanter, *Men and Women of the Corporation* (New York: Basic Books, 1977).
[7] Norma Briggs, "Women Apprentices: Removing the Barriers," *Manpower*, Vol. 6, No. 12 (December 1974), pp. 3–11.

Sociologists are only now beginning to read the sex map of the work world and to recognize that most jobs are sex-stereotyped. Briggs recommends that one way to change that reality is to change the way we talk about it. Job titles should be changed, she argues, to omit the inference of sex stereotypes. In the 1977 edition of the *DOT*, job titles give no indication of age and sex.[8] Craftsmen are now known as craft workers, salesmen as sales workers, clergymen as clergy. And people receive, not workmen's compensation but workers' compensation.

The Quiet Revolution

If researchers ignored women workers, society as a whole appeared to be making the same error. The change in the sex composition of the workforce that came about in one generation—from 1952, when women made up less than 33 percent of the workforce, to 1977, when the proportion rose to 41 percent—was little heralded. The Women's Bureau of the Department of Labor summarized the nature of the change by comparing the typical woman worker of 1920 with her counterpart in 1970. (See Table 1.)

Why has this change come about? Many explanations have been advanced. Perhaps the least persuasive is that which attributes women's increased economic activity to the women's liberation movement. Feminists are, it is said, driving women out of the home. A second popular explanation is that women are bored: modern appliances make housework so easy that women work to fill the time their grandmothers spent keeping house. There is little evidence to support either of these claims.

The increase can more logically be attributed to the lowered birth rate, the increase in women's education, the longer life expectancy, the rising divorce rate, and, most persuasive of all, rising expectations about what constitutes a good life. We do not need to speculate about why single

---

[8] Don Barnes, "20,000 Jobs," *Worklife*, Vol. 3, No. 2 (February 1978), pp. 9–13.

Table 1. The typical American woman worker.

	1920	1970
Background		
Percentage of the workforce comprised of women	20%	38%
Percentage of women of working age who were employed	23%	49%
Specifics		
Age	28	39
Marital status	Single	Married
Occupation	Factory work	Clerical work
Life expectancy	55 years	75 years
Work life expectancy	17 years	23 years

Source: Adapted from *Women Workers Today* (Washington, D.C.: U.S. Department of Labor, 1974 rev.), pp. 1–8.

women and women who are the sole support of their families work—they always have. The married woman, the mother of small children, is the newcomer whose presence needs to be explained. She has fewer children than her grandmother did, she will have a longer life after her children are in school, and she has invested more in her own education. A mother may want her children to have more than she had and may find that one salary is not enough to send them to college. Or it may be that one paycheck (though of course higher in dollars and in real wages than it was in, say, 1945) does not go far enough toward duplicating the lifestyle Americans are encouraged to aspire to. In any case, the married woman's major impetus appears to be, not any desire to actualize herself as a "liberated feminist" or to fill up empty hours but a desire to earn money she feels she needs.

What jobs do women do? First it is helpful to analyze the total American workforce. The Bureau of Labor Statistics classifies occupations into nine general families, representing some 96.1 million jobholders.[9]

[9] *Employment and Earnings* (Washington, D.C.: U.S. Department of Labor, B.L.S., Sept. 1978), Vol. 25, No. 9, p. 35.

The percentage of the American workforce in each of these groups in 1978 was as follows:

Professional, technical	14%
Managerial, administrative	11
Sales	6
Clerical	18
Craft workers	14
Operatives	15
Laborers	6
Service workers	14
Farm workers	2
	100%

The distribution of male and female workers among these occupational families is shown in Table 2. It can be seen that women hold a disproportionate share of clerical and service jobs; they are underrepresented in a number of categories, including skilled craft work and managerial and administrative jobs.

Table 2. The American workforce, by sex and occupation, 1978.

Occupational Group	Male Workforce	Female Workforce
Professional and technical	14%	15%
Managerial and administrative	14	6
Sales	6	7
Clerical	6	35
Craft workers	21	2
Operatives	17	12
Laborers	9	1
Service	9	21
Farm	4	1
	100%	100%

Source: *Employment and Earnings* (Washington, D.C.: U.S. Department of Labor, B.L.S., Sept. 1978), Vol. 25, No. 9, p. 35.

This imbalance, seen by some as ordained by nature and irreversible, is the source of unease for feminists, in part because of the increasing gap between wages earned by women and those earned by men. In the United States in 1977, women as a group earned only 58 percent of the wages earned by men, down from 62 percent in 1967. The pay gap is greatest in the occupational category of saleswork, where, even though men and women may share the same title, they sell far different commodities. Whereas men may sell machines, appliances, or cars, women are by and large confined to selling women's clothes and cosmetics.

Indeed, there is no occupational family where women's earnings are equal to men's. According to the Women's Bureau, in 1973 women's earnings as a percentage of men's earnings were as follows:

Professional and technical	66%
Managerial and administrative	59
Clerical	60
Sales Workers	41
Operatives	58
Service Workers	60

As we shall see, men are in a far wider range of occupations than women are. In general, "masculine" occupations offer a greater likelihood of high reward in terms of prestige, pay, promotion, and security.

Some researchers attribute the disparity in occupations and the resulting pay gap to women's pattern of labor force participation over their lives. Many women enter the workforce at approximately the same age as their brothers, but they do not persist until retirement. Instead, they take off years from work to care for small children, reentering at some point after their services are not so needed at home. This "childbearing lapse" proves to be quite expensive in terms of lifetime earnings, not only because of the income forgone but because of the formidable barriers at reentry.

Among the problems women encounter when they seek to go back to work are lack of current skills, lack of knowledge of the range of jobs available, and, perhaps most crippling, a dearth of self-confidence. This "collapse of confidence" often leads middle-aged women to accept positions below their capability in terms of education, experience, and potential.

Some attribute women's lower average earnings to the greater likelihood of their seeking or accepting part-time work, work close to home, or part-year employment. An explanation that used to be widely accepted—that women have less access to education than men and thus are confined to lower-paying jobs—is not supported by evidence. Working women and men have approximately the same median years of schooling. The sad fact is that women with master's degrees are, on average, earning less than men who dropped out of high school. In 1973, according to the Women's Bureau, year-round full-time women workers with one to three years of high school earned an average of $5,513; men in this group earned $10,401. Among workers with four or more years of college, average earnings were $9,771 for women and $16,576 for men.

Why do women earn so much less than men? Why do they enter such a narrow range of occupations? The answers lie deep in our beliefs about what is appropriate behavior for a girl and for a boy. So long as girls are encouraged to pursue "feminine" interests exclusively (and boys, "masculine" interests), and so long as young people act on those impulses, we will have a balkanized workforce where some jobs are seen as suitable for males and others for females.

The Counterrevolution

It has been suggested that the women's liberation movement has no direct link with women's increasing participation in the workforce. What is clear is that the renewed interest in women's rights in the late 1960s has had an impact on public policy. As surely as the granting of suffrage to women in 1920 can be traced to the first women's rights convention in 1848 in Seneca Falls, so the antidiscrimination legislation of the 1970s can be traced to pressure from a new generation of feminists.

As some women awoke from what feminist leader Kate Millett called their "long sleep," they began to recognize that even though some of their sisters were quite content with "women's lot," others were not. Those who were trying to enter jobs traditionally held by men faced insurmountable barriers. Women were encountering sex-based discrimination in the workplace, as in the larger society. In the early 1970s the journal *Psychology Today* ran a cover symbolizing women's problems in a society where they were alleged to be equal with men. The cover showed two runners poised at the beginning of a footrace. The man was dressed in track shorts; his eyes were fixed ahead and he looked eager to be off. The woman looked equally eager but it was clear that her performance might be hindered. She had a baby in a knapsack on her back and a dog on a leash. It would have been appropriate to picture her balancing a tray of food and a bag of laundry as well. Equal at the start? Indeed.

The idea that women's problems originate at home may well be grounded in fact. But it is also a fact that work organizations have perpetuated the situation and profited from it. It may be that personnel managers are bearing an unfair burden, being expected to right wrongs that did not originate with them. But rightly or wrongly, personnel managers now have the clear obligation to obey the laws enacted to protect women and make them more nearly equal to men at the start of the footrace.

The Remedies: Antidiscrimination Laws

The Fourteenth Amendment to the U.S. Constitution provides that "no state shall . . . deny to any person within its jurisdiction the equal protection of the laws." If women are people, it would seem that they already have constitutional protection of their equal rights. But by custom and policy women have been treated so differently from men that the "equal protection" doctrine has not been invoked to protect them as it has their brothers.[10] Three important general federal laws have been enacted to protect women:

■ *The Equal Pay Act of 1963*, an amendment to the Fair Labor Standards Act, went into effect in June 1964. The law is administered by the Wage and Hours Division of the Department of Labor. Employers are prohibited from paying women and men different wages when they do jobs that are the same or similar in skill, effort, and responsibility, and that are performed under similar working conditions. The act covers employers and unions in industries engaged in interstate commerce.

■ *Title VII of the Civil Rights Act of 1964*, as amended in 1972, resulted in the creation of the Equal Employment Opportunity Commission (EEOC). The legislation bans discrimination on the basis of race, color, religion, sex, or national origin in hiring, referral, classification, membership in labor organizations, admission to apprenticeships, and other terms and conditions of employment. Also prohibited under Title VII are advertisements that indicate discriminatory preferences. The legislation covers employers of 15 or more workers, employment agencies, labor organizations, and joint labor–management apprenticeship committees.

■ *The Age Discrimination in Employment Act of 1967*, effective in June 1968, is administered by the Secretary of Labor. The law prohibits discrimination against people between the ages of 40 and 65 in hiring, referral, classification, compensation, and other terms and conditions of employment (and related advertising) on the part of employers with 25 or more workers, employment agencies, and labor organizations.

Additional legislation has been enacted to provide specific protection to certain groups:

[10] Ruth Bader Ginsburg, "The Equal Rights Amendment Is the Way," *Harvard Women's Law Journal*, Vol. 1, No. 1 (Spring 1978), pp. 24–25.

■ *Executive Order 11246* (1965), as amended by *Executive Order 11375* (1968), covers employers with federal contracts or subcontracts of more than $10,000. The law not only bans discrimination against applicants and employees on the basis of race, color, religion, sex, or national origin; it also requires that employers "take affirmative action" to insure the provision of equal opportunity. Further, employers must state in all advertising that they are indeed affirmative action/equal opportunity employers. According to Revised Order 4, employers with over $50,000 in federal contracts and 50 or more workers must file affirmative action plans with goals and timetables with the Office of Federal Contract Compliance.

■ *The Rehabilitation Act of 1973* prohibits discrimination on the basis of physical or mental impairment by employers with federal contracts greater than $2,500. Administered by the Interagency Commission on Handicapped Employment, the law requires that employers take affirmative action to insure provision of equal opportunity to the handicapped.

■ *Title IX of the Education Amendments Act of 1972,* effective July 1975, bans discrimination on the basis of sex in all federally assisted education programs. Administered through the Department of Labor by the Department of Health, Education, and Welfare, the law covers public and private preschools, elementary and secondary schools, vocational and professional schools, graduate schools of higher education, and public undergraduate institutions of higher education.

In March 1972, in its report "Guidelines on Discrimination Because of Sex," the EEOC set forth general principles to assist employers in complying with Title VII of the Civil Rights Act. Employers could not refuse to hire a woman because they believed women in general have a higher turnover rate than men do. Nor could they refuse to hire a woman because of the assumption that women as a group are less capable at certain tasks than men are. Nor could employers cite the preferences of co-workers or customers in excluding women (or men) from consideration for

employment. The guidelines also provide the useful information that Title VII supersedes state laws that treat
women workers differently from men. And the guidelines
provide clarification as to the illegality of separate seniority
systems by sex, discrimination against married women,
sex-separated advertising, discriminatory practices by
employment agencies, preemployment inquiries by sex,
provision of unequal fringe benefits, and provision of discriminatory benefits for temporary disabilities, such as
those related to pregnancy and childbirth.

Affirmative Action: Is It Helping?

The federal laws are in place; in addition, some states
have passed legislation that is even more specific in its protection. The requirement that employers act affirmatively
with respect to women of all races (and minority men) can
be defined much more simply than in the language of the
legislation itself. The laws require not merely that
employers stop any illegal discriminatory practices but also
that they take positive action—for example, that they make
a special effort to include women and minorities among
those who are reached by their job advertisements. If
employers make a good-faith effort to seek out, hire, and
promote women and minority group men on the same basis
as majority members are sought, hired, and promoted, they
will be in compliance with both the letter and the spirit of
the legislation.

Have these laws assisted women? The question is difficult to answer; indeed, the answers differ with the point of
view of the respondent. A study comparing the sex and race
composition of companies that were visited by compliance
officers versus companies that were not, suggested that
affirmative action programs were helping men—especially
white men—but having an adverse effect on women.[11]

[11] Morris Goldstein and Robert S. Smith, "The Estimated Impact of the
Antidiscrimination Program Aimed at Federal Contractors," *Industrial
and Labor Relations Review*, Vol. 29, No. 4 (July 1976), pp. 523–543.

Similarly, a review of the status of women and minorities in administrative posts in institutions of higher education showed that despite professed commitment, little progress had been made by 1976.[12] Another researcher suggested that the excess of government regulations applying to academic institutions has acted as a damper to change rather than fanning it.[13] Reviews of women's occupational status at all levels show a widening of the pay gap, infinitesimal progress in crossing sex lines in jobs, and increasing unemployment among women.

In some cases, an excess of zeal on the part of employers may be hindering progress. One of the nation's biggest employers of women found that overenthusiastic compliance (or overcompliance) made matters worse. The directive from top management stipulated that those hiring explain their actions in writing whenever they passed over women applicants on a "short list" in favor of white males. Managers who might have included women among the last few candidates for an opening found themselves cutting some women out of the running altogether. This was (by their own admission) to avoid the additional complications of having to explain on special forms in lengthy detail why the women were not suited to the job. Another of the nation's big companies found itself adopting a cynical attitude toward compliance when officers visited. A black officer who visited would emphasize minorities; a female compliance officer who was a member of an ethnic group would stress the representation of her people in the corporate workforce.

Some feminists think of affirmative action as a joke—and a bad one at that. It seems ironic to them that employers should be permitted to advertise themselves as acting affirmatively when the underrepresentation of women in top jobs and their prevalence in low-paid service jobs continues

[12] Carol Van Alstyne et al., "Affirmative Inaction: The Bottom Line Tells the Tale," *Change,* Vol. 9, No. 8 (August 1977), pp. 39–41.

[13] D. C. Spriestersbach and William J. Farrell, "Impact of Federal Regulations at a University," *Science,* Vol. 198, No. 4312 (October 7, 1977), pp. 27–30.

unchanged. This is seen as evidence that affirmative action programs are not working, and are not meant to be. If equal employment specialists are set up in a special unit, the corporation is criticized for detoothing the program by segregating the experts away from the action. If the responsibility of providing equal opportunity is distributed among the staff and line units, the company is accused of putting the responsibility for monitoring progress and erasing discrimination in the very place where discrimination originates and is perpetuated. A final cynical view is expressed by a women's recruitment specialist who dismisses all corporate efforts as "cosmetic." Behind that corporate mask, she writes, there is clear evidence that employers want to keep women out and to do the bare minimum to appear to be complying with the law.[14]

The incredible increase in women's participation in the workforce is a fact of American life. Just as tangible are the new laws seeking to protect them. Many citizens sneered when the Department of Health, Education, and Welfare sought to outlaw father–son banquets. More recently, the HEW ruling that at schools in Oak Ridge, Tennessee, "it will also be necessary that varsity cheerleaders cheer equally loudly for both boys' and girls' varsity teams" prompted one journalist to remark that the federal brow should not be knit with such concerns: "No government can afford to act stupidly and make the public irritable. Certainly a government that talks about the moral equivalent of war should not squander solemnity on cheerleaders." [15] A Register and Tribune syndicated cartoon published in 1976 expressed a similar sentiment. It showed government officials chortling as they tapped out a lengthy directive to the effect that families with but one child must take affirmative action to correct the implicit sexual imbalance. We can look forward, perhaps, to guidelines on just how this can be done.

[14] Frances Lear, "EEO Compliance: Behind the Corporate Mask," *Harvard Business Review*, Vol. 53, No. 4 (July–August 1975), pp. 138–146.
[15] George F. Will, "People Are Fed Up with HEW's Rules," *Ithaca (N.Y.) Journal*, March 6, 1978, p. 12.

While it is clear that there is cynicism (and grounds for it) among corporate officials and feminists alike about the present state of affirmative action programs, it would be frivolous to let cynics have the last word. Obviously, major changes in social policy cannot take place without trouble and confusion. In 1973, the American Telephone and Telegraph Company, threatened with a lawsuit, signed a consent agreement with the EEOC, promising to take many affirmative steps to ensure equal employment opportunities for women of all races and minority men. The cost, estimated at well over $60 million, suggested that the company feared an even more unfavorable outcome if the lawsuit had been allowed to proceed.[16] Phyllis Wallace, a professor at MIT's Alfred P. Sloan School of Management, has noted that AT&T has been permanently changed by its agreement with the EEOC in 1973. Wallace, author of a book about the AT&T case, says, "Women and minorities are now in positions where they will keep putting pressure on the company. They will file charges or threaten to file. You can't go backwards." [17]

[16] Ruth Gilbert Shaeffer, "Improving Job Opportunities for Women—From a U.S. Corporate Perspective, 1970–1975," (New York: The Conference Board, 1978), p. 1 and footnote 4, p. 40.

[17] Georgette Jasen, "Ma Bell's Daughters," *The Wall Street Journal,* February 28, 1978, p. 1.

Company policy is fantastic. It's
motherhood, apple pie, the flag. But
that policy is implemented by people,
and some of them carry around a lot of
baggage from the past.
*—An engineering staff specialist
at AT&T headquarters* [1]

2

The Personnel
Department's
Responsibility

"THE purpose of the personnel department," says a newly
hired assistant, "is to serve as the conscience of the organization. When somebody in top management proposes a new
system of getting the work out or a new procedure for controlling quality, we in personnel have to ask, 'But how will
this affect the people?' Our job is looking out for them."
When she said that, she had had her bachelor's degree (and
her job) for only six months. The definition may have a
blue-sky quality to older, wiser practitioners who have

[1] Georgette Jasen, "Ma Bell's Daughters," *The Wall Street Journal*,
February 28, 1978, p. 1.

been in place long enough to know that their work often involves just keeping the ship afloat or putting out fires. They may predict that the newly arrived practitioner who sees herself solely as a change agent may in fact only change management's mind about the wisdom of hiring her. But this new assistant does recognize a level of activity that is sometimes overlooked by those who see the personnel department as the dumping ground for staff members who can't make it on the line.

A director of personnel at a research organization recently remarked that assistants to top managers may in fact share the view that personnel work has a lower priority than matters having to do with production. "When the new president was appointed," he said, "I had some trouble getting past his assistants to talk with him. I always remember the day when they told me he was too busy, had to meet on important matters with department heads, and so forth. Finally, I said, 'Look, I have to get to him about a couple of things. One is this matter of his benefits. If we don't get that straightened out, he won't get a pay check this month.' It was funny how fast I got in then. And no trouble after that either."

The Nature of the Personnel Function

One useful definition of the personnel function as a whole uses a typology of four levels of work. Level 1 work (the lowest) includes recordkeeping and other important but routine duties involved in keeping the organization operating. Level 2 work involves more responsibility; it requires serving as an organizational buffer, helping to resolve disputes between staff and staff and management and staff. Level 3 duties are more challenging in that they involve anticipating and dealing with situations before they become Level 2 problems. At this level, personnel practitioners are serving as watchdogs on both management and workers and as an early warning system, anticipating problems. Level 4 tasks are those involved in consulting on company policy.[2] The newcomer quoted above was considering Level 4 work as the primary purpose of the personnel function. Not a bad goal at which to aim.

The range of personnel activities at each of the four levels can be deduced from the sample job titles provided by a recent text on personnel management: [3]

Personnel director
Director of industrial relations
Employment manager
Compensation analyst
Benefits coordinator
Job analyst
Personnel interviewer
Personnel research analyst
Labor relations specialist
Safety coordinator
Employee relations counselor
Corporate ombudsman
EEO compliance manager
Training director
Manager of organization development
Pension analyst
Employee services coordinator
Testing consultant

This list is not exhaustive. Perhaps the only important omission is the title of vice president for personnel. Researchers have noted that presidents of companies are seldom drawn from the ranks of personnel work. But vice presidents for personnel relations often are. Still, their numbers are limited. New graduates like the one quoted earlier should be aware that in this field entry-level jobs are comparatively accessible. There are opportunities for promotion, but the career ladder to top management is a narrow one.

If, as Foulkes and Morgan suggest, it is top managers who make policy and line managers who implement it, then

[2] William J. Wasmuth et al., *Human Resource Administration: Problems of Growth and Change* (Boston: Houghton Mifflin, 1970), p. 10.
[3] Robert L. Mathis and John H. Jackson, *Personnel: Contemporary Perspectives and Applications* (St. Paul, Minn.: West, 1976), p. 423.

the specialists and generalists in personnel are those who audit and control and who have, as well, the opportunity to innovate. But they often get bogged down in routine service work.[4] So our newcomer is in part correct. She may, in fact, serve as an innovator, if top management permits experimentation. A project she develops may serve as a model for programs adopted throughout the company.

But in personnel, as elsewhere, she may find herself handicapped by her sex. The first professional-level jobs in industry open to women were in personnel. At the turn of the century, the field was devoted almost entirely to "welfare" concerns; many aspects of it were seen as suitable for women. With the coming of World War I, the field became more differentiated and technical and men moved into personnel work. Where women had been welcomed as matrons, social secretaries, coordinators of educational programs, and guardians of the health and welfare of workers, men were seemingly preferred for jobs such as legal advisors, efficiency and time-and-motion experts, and salary administrators.[5]

In the 1960s and 1970s the personnel function in many companies was relabeled the Human Resources Department or Human Development Services. This would appear to be a reversion to an earlier philosophy when personnel was viewed essentially as a "sunshine committee." But the new emphasis is not reflected in the sex composition of personnel departments (however they are named), which are nearly as traditional as line units in terms of differentiation of jobs by sex.

Most aspects of personnel work have to do with managing human resources—that is, managing the people already on staff and attempting to match their talents to the jobs that

---

[4] Fred K. Foulkes and Henry K. Morgan, "Organizing and Staffing the Personnel Function," *Harvard Business Review*, Vol. 55, No. 3 (May–June 1977), p. 144.

[5] Frank B. Miller and Mary Ann Coghill, "Sex and the Personnel Manager," *Industrial and Labor Relations Review*, Vol. 18, No. 1 (October 1964), pp. 32–44.

need to be done. Later chapters will analyze the three aspects of personnel work that appear to be affected most by the new legislation: recruitment, selection, and training. Ultimately, of course, all phases will be changed. Many feminists hope that time will come sooner rather than later. They are pressing for change in the administration of retirement benefits so that men and women who pay the same amount into the plan receive equal monthly payments after retirement; for recognition of the fact that maternity leave is, despite what some court decisions suggest, an issue intimately and irrevocably linked to sex-based discrimination; and for some corporate and government assistance in providing child care facilities for working parents. At this writing, however, the laws and guidelines are most specific in the three areas of recruitment, selection, and training. Those requirements are sweeping enough, some feel. For instance, the requirement for affirmative recruitment means that management must concern itself not only with present employees but with people outside, especially those who in a sense "should be on the payroll."

To summarize the advantages and disadvantages of choosing to pursue personnel work: Personnel is an expanding field, but it is hard for managers to reach the top. The field is growing in prestige and influence, but it still suffers from an old image as the department where low producers can be dumped. Part of the image problem is inherent in the nature of the work, being staff instead of line.

The personnel department can be influential in an organization, but it should not be imagined that all practitioners can be innovators, at least at the entry level. Finally, women who choose careers in the personnel field should be aware that their sex is better represented there than in many other occupations (in part a carryover from earlier times when worker welfare concerns were paramount). At the same time, they should recognize that today women hold only 2.5 percent of the personnel jobs paying $25,000 a year or more.

The Responsibility to Act Affirmatively

The specific nature of the responsibility to act affirmatively can be deduced from the steps involved in setting up an affirmative action plan. The work organization should concern itself with:

1. Analyzing its current workforce to ascertain the sex and race composition of the workers at each job level.
2. Analyzing the availability of those groups not fully integrated into the national workforce and therefore the focus of concern: women and members of certain minority groups.
3. Ascertaining, from steps 1 and 2, to what extent the company is "underutilizing" women of all races and minority men.
4. Setting goals and target dates for correcting the underutilization.
5. Auditing progress toward reaching the goals.
6. Expanding the advertisement of job openings to encourage applications from members of underutilized groups.
7. Developing and encouraging participation in training programs.
8. Reviewing the company's responsibility toward community service.[6]

Companies may find themselves criticized from within at each step. For some years, in fact, universities were stalled at step 1. Their personnel policies were such that they had a great deal of difficulty in complying with federal directives that required analysis of their own workforce. Hiring was so decentralized, recordkeeping so casual, and the sources of funds flowing through the universities so diverse that presidents were hard pressed to report how

[6] Adapted from *Affirmative Action and Equal Employment: A Guidebook for Employers* (Washington, D.C.: U.S. Equal Employment Opportunity Commission, 1974), Vol. 1, pp. 16–63.

many faculty members they had, never mind how they might be distributed by sex and race.

One problem arose from the rapid growth of many educational institutions after World War II. The number of students, faculty, and staff grew much faster than the personnel departments. A second difficulty arose because of the nature of the academic enterprise. Faculty members found themselves expected to act as "managers" of employees (their research assistants and clerical help) when they had thought of themselves as members of an academic community, scholars who came together to teach the young the fruits of the research they pursued. Threats of withdrawal of federal funds from the institution had little impact on some professors, whose first loyalty was not to the institution as such but to their disciplines. Other professors were unmoved by legal pressures because they genuinely did not know how much their institutions depended on federal funds for research support.

In any case, universities had problems in analyzing the nature of their workers, in part because they thought of themselves as educators primarily and employers only by accident. A further complication arose because some faculty members felt that the university should not be identifying its employees by sex and race, no matter how high the motive or how pressing the legal obligation. They took the position that for the purpose of recordkeeping, nobody should be labeled. To drive that point home, one department chairman assured his listeners in a public forum that he was sex-blind and race-blind. "We hire the best," he asserted. "Our department has one Italian, two Americans of German descent, three of British heritage." The danger of that high-minded posture is that it can easily be misunderstood when the department consists, as his did, entirely of white males. The personnel practitioner must respond to such an assertion in the spirit that Supreme Court Justice John Marshall Harlan did in 1896: "Our constitution is color-blind. But until our society translates that ideal into everyday practice, the decision maker who is color-blind is blind to injustice." Except that since 1896 we have added sex-blindness to race-blindness as an affliction to be cured rather than a state to be sought.

Beliefs about Women Workers

In 1918, the first program to train managers in personnel was undertaken in Rochester, New York. Eight topics were studied by the apprentice managers: complaints, suggestion systems, safety practices, labor recruiting, recreation, interviewing techniques, medical exams, and women workers.[7] These subspecialties within personnel still are themes for training. Some critics of American business and industry point to health and safety as the area where employers need the most education or legal pressure to serve workers' needs. Other critics see the fundamental problem as the lack of worker participation in decision making, a weakness inherent in the capitalist system. Few can deny, however, that the problems of women workers have been overlooked. As was noted in Chapter 1, the labor force participation of women has increased drastically in a generation.

But this reality is little known. In children's books women are by and large still pictured at home.[8] Men are shown in a wide range of occupations, but women remain in the kitchen. They are seldom even shown driving a car, something a suburban mother does quite often indeed. A study of the image of women on television undertaken by sociologist Gaye Tuchman at Queens College shows that that powerful medium is also transmitting an outdated image. In 1952, 32 percent of the working people shown on TV were women. By 1970, that proportion had gone down to 20 percent; five years later, it had not changed.

[7] Miller and Coghill, pp. 38 ff.
[8] Lenore Weitzman et al., "Sex Role Socialization in Picture Books for Preschool Children," *American Journal of Sociology*, Vol. 77, No. 6 (May 1972), pp. 1125–1150.

Perhaps it should not be a surprise that little girls consistently anticipate spending most of their lives out of the workforce. They surely lack role models, since working women are so seldom seen in the media. One researcher suggests that this general dearth of models may well account for the popularity of Gothic novels among American women. These romantic paperback books—whose covers often feature a woman in a long dress fleeing from a castle—may not be the ultimate in realism, but they do show women as independent, strong-minded individuals who defy conventional "feminine" norms and take responsibility for their own lives.[9] Perhaps the most depressing research note on role models in the mass media comes from a study of Carolyn Keene's novels about the adventures of Nancy Drew. For all her independence and skill at solving mysteries, Nancy was still the victim of her time. Not only was she a racist, the analysis concludes, but she was not a real feminist in terms of advocating equality between the sexes.[10] A symbol, perhaps, of how the mighty have fallen is the fact that the last volume published in the Nancy Drew series was a cookbook.

Even Nancy Drew succumbed to the pervasive American belief that woman's place is in the home. Boys are still reared for work and girls for marriage. Distinctions are made from the moment of birth: baby girls are wrapped in pink blankets, baby boys in blue. Girls are given names of flowers and jewels, or diminutives of male names (Paula, Charlotte); boys are often given treasured family names, especially those thought to sound strong and "masculine." Drugstores carry dictionaries of names to help parents choose. One popular version is, of course, divided into two sections: boys and girls. The first section is preceded by the following verse:

   [9] Josephine A. Ruggiero and Louise C. Weston, "Sex Role Characterization of Women in 'Modern Gothic' Novels," *Pacific Sociological Review,* Vol. 20, No. 2 (April 1977), pp. 279–300.
   [10] Bobbie Ann Mason, *The Girl Sleuth* (Old Westbury, N.Y.: Feminist Press, 1975).

The name that polls the winning votes
The famous name that makes up quotes
The name with thousands in employ
Will be the name you name your boy.

The second section is introduced as follows:

She'll be made of sunshine, sugar, and spice
She'll be pert and pretty and awfully nice
Someday she'll have to change her name.
Now choose the one that will stay the same.[11]

Clearly, we accept (often unthinkingly) quite disparate ideals for girls and for boys. Certain beliefs about women workers are likewise widely accepted. In 1973 the Women's Bureau of the Department of Labor listed nine such beliefs:

1. A woman's place is in the home.
2. Women aren't seriously attached to the labor force; they work only for pocket money.
3. Women are out ill more than male workers; they cost the company more.
4. Women don't work as long or as regularly as their male co-workers; their training is costly—and largely wasted.
5. Married women take jobs away from men; in fact, they ought to quit the jobs they now hold.
6. Women should stick to "women's jobs" and shouldn't compete for "men's jobs."
7. Women don't want responsibility on the job; they don't want promotions or job changes that add to their load.
8. The employment of mothers leads to juvenile delinquency.
9. Men don't like to work for women supervisors.

[11] *3,500 Names for Baby* (New York: Dell, 1976).

The Women's Bureau deemed each of these assertions a myth.[12] Additional research evidence published since 1973 suggests that the issues are more complicated than simply labeling the statements true or false.

Assertion 1, that "woman's place is in the home," is more a statement of belief about where women should be than a statement of where they are. The fact is that most American women do keep house, but a great many of them work for pay outside the home as well. As we saw in Chapter 1, half the women of working age now work. Whether they should or not is a matter of opinion and not fact.

Assertion 2, that women are not seriously attached to the workforce, is true in that women do take time off to bear children and to stay with them when they are young. Current data show, however, that more and more mothers of young children are having (or choosing) to stay on in the workforce. As we know, women's work life expectancy *is* shorter than men's, despite the increase in the number of working mothers. The allusion to "pocket money" is likewise misleading, since at least 60 percent of women who work for pay appear to have no choice, in that they have no man to support them.

Assertion 3, about days lost from work, is likewise true in part. The data show that women as a group do lose slightly more time than men. But when the evidence is sorted by job level, the differences disappear. In other words, men and women in comparable jobs lose comparable numbers of days at work. Highly paid workers in high-prestige jobs lose fewer days than service workers. The comparatively few women in top jobs lose as few days as the many men at that level. The many women bunched at the bottom of the pay scales are staying home sick virtually the same number of days as the men at that level. The most recent study of sex differences in time worked shows persuasive evidence that women workers at all levels studied

[12] *The Myth and The Reality* (Washington, D.C.: U.S. Department of Labor, 1974 rev.).

in fact spend more clock hours actually working than their male co-workers. (See Chapter 9.)

Assertion 4, that women do not work as long or as regularly as men, is closely related to assertion 2. It too is a half-truth, for the same reasons.

Assertion 5, that married women take jobs away from men, is clearly an absurdity in some respects. As the Women's Bureau points out, in 1973 more than 19 million employed women were married. The number of unemployed men was a fraction of that: 3.1 million. So the married women who would nobly stay home to provide work for unemployed men would leave some 16 million jobs unfilled. In fact, a match would clearly be difficult to achieve, since men hold far different jobs than women do. So the two groups are seldom in competition.

The implication of the assertion is, however, that it is not fair for some families to have two salaries while others have none. That injustice, like the uneven distribution of wealth among Americans, can be argued about but not labeled true or false.

Assertion 6, that women should stick to "women's jobs," is likewise a statement of belief about how people ought to behave. Indeed, women traditionally have sought women's jobs and men, men's. Nothing in the new laws holds them back from continuing to do so. But the law now requires that "ability to do the work" be the determining factor in hiring, not sex or race.

Assertion 7, that women don't want responsibility on the job—with its implication that women already carry a heavy burden if they care for a family and work for pay—is likewise true in part. But women without families often seek challenging jobs; sometimes women with small children and many responsibilities at home are more ambitious than their male co-workers.

Assertion 8 links maternal employment with juvenile delinquency. This association did appear in some of the research evidence that was accepted in the 1960s. But researchers, seeking to understand those findings, have come to realize that many of the studies confounded numerous factors that contribute to delinquent behavior and singled out maternal employment unfairly. More recent studies suggest that the quality of time a mother spends with her child is more important than the quantity. Similarly, the mother's acceptance of her situation appears to be an important influence. While some young wives may feel deprived at having to be away from their children part of each working day, others may believe that they have found the best possible solution to the dilemma that a woman often confronts. She is made to choose between devotion to family and the development of a serious full-time career, a choice no man is expected to make.

Assertion 9, that men don't like to work for women supervisors, is probably true. The editors of *Esquire* go so far as to say that "working for a female boss is driving some men to drink." [13] A study undertaken in an early women's studies course in 1970 uncovered evidence that even those students who were different from their peers in that they had chosen to enroll in a course on women favored men teachers over women and men bosses over women. But this attitude may be changing.

The Women's Bureau notes that most men who say they would not like to report to a woman have never done so. Few have. But there is evidence that some women bosses are not effective, just as some men bosses are not. Similarly, some women bosses are evaluated favorably, as are some men bosses. The commonsense answer is that workers want good bosses—a desire that, it is hoped, overrides sex preferences. One aspect of being a "good boss" may well be the ability to wield power on behalf of subordinates. Since women so often hold organizational jobs with limited opportunity to wield influence, their desirability as bosses may be curtailed. That too may change as (and if) more women make their way up the corporate ladder.

[13] "Backstage with Esquire," *Esquire*, Vol. 89, No. 5 (March 28, 1978), p. 5.

Data show that men who report to women tend to conceal that fact in social settings, almost as though their manhood were diminished by it. This finding adds credence to sociologist Theodore Caplow's assertion that two beliefs are deeply embedded in our psyches: that the sexes should be separate at work and that women should not supervise men.[14]

Male/Female Differences

Clearly, it is difficult to generalize about half the human race. Research is only now beginning to come in that will permit us to label certain generalizations as myths. It is safer to reject all such sweeping statements than to accept them. And basing employment decisions on them is not only unwise but in some cases illegal.

Proponents of the new legislation are often accused of ignoring the biological reality that women bear children and men don't. "Vive la différence!" goes the argument. Men (and women) who fear changes in sex role differentiation argue that women need special protection, not equal treatment. Harking back to hunting-gathering societies, they speak of the average man's greater strength and join with Lionel Tiger, author of *Men in Groups,* in attributing women's absence from public life to natural causes. Men, according to Tiger, have an inborn trait that leads them to bond together with other men in fraternities, social clubs, war parties, and political alliances. Women, he asserts, do not bond together well.

Women's studies researchers are the first to admit that men and women are different as groups. Linguists can distinguish tape recordings of baby boys' and baby girls' "babbling" as early as six months of age. Girl students tend to carry their schoolbooks quite differently from boy stu-

[14] Theodore Caplow, *The Sociology of Work* (New York: McGraw-Hill, 1964), p. 238.

dents. In high schools the graffiti on the walls of the girls' room are different in theme and frequency from the graffiti in the boys' room.

Last year, undergraduates learning research methods undertook to tabulate some 6,000 pictures of graduating seniors in yearbooks. They recognized the problems of comparing pictures from the 1950s with those of the 1960s and in turn with those of the 1970s. They compared college yearbooks with high school annuals. There were problems in definition: how to distinguish a grin from a grimace? Does a half-smile count?

After resolving those differences and agreeing on what they were looking for, they set about to count. They ascertained that about a third of the men were pictured smiling versus a little over half the women. When they sought an explanation for this sex difference, they significantly did not choose a biological one. It could have been, they reasoned, that the photographer encouraged girls more than boys to smile, or that the girls chose proofs that showed them smiling more often than the boys did. Each of these could be due in fact to social explanations having to do with group beliefs about appropriate behavior for each sex.

These undergraduates and the people who teach them are coming to be suspicious of biological explanations of the differences between the sexes in any attitude, behavior, talent, or aptitude. Young people are asking hard questions. If women are innately good at nurturing behavior, why aren't they hearing confessions as Catholic priests? If women are by nature good at delicate tasks such as wiring television sets, why aren't they dentists and surgeons? If nature intended man to be woman's protector, why are men dying seven years sooner than their female counterparts, leaving their wives when they are most in need of protection?

We cannot know how society would be organized if the similarities rather than differences between males and females were emphasized from childhood. It is virtually impossible to predict whether our political system would be different if women had an equal voice in controlling it.

Would women physicians change the health care system to make it more sensitive to women's needs? If women made policy for corporations in the United States, would the workplace be more humane? Impossible to say. If women were encouraged to participate in active sports and develop their bodies from an early age, women as a group might come much, much closer to men as a group in terms of physical strength. They might. If our definitions of appropriate "feminine" behavior were drastically modified, women might be as likely to choose serious careers in scientific fields that would lead them to line jobs in industrial organizations, instead of being disproportionately grouped in service, clerical, and other staff jobs such as posts in personnel where they work with "people problems." Perhaps this will come to pass. If women were not expected to achieve security through marriage but to earn their own way, more young people might choose to marry at leisure and not find themselves repenting at haste. The birth rate might go down, but each child might be a wanted one. The security of two incomes would give both women and men more freedom in choosing work they find compatible and rewarding. All these things might happen. And they might not.

Meantime, we have little solid evidence that women are fundamentally different from men except in the matter of their ability to conceive, bear, and nurse babies. To be sure, men and women have been raised differently. We will never know, perhaps, how much of the difference is due to nature and how much to nurture until we live in a society where we truly nurture individual talents without regard to sex. In any case, it is clear that neither sex has a corner on one trait: gullibility.

For hundreds of years, we have been telling one another things about the nature of masculinity and femininity and perhaps making one another miserable either because we did not live up to the sex role ideals or because our sex (whichever one) did not match up to the other. Some businessmen still believe that when women are menstruating they are dirtier than usual or can tarnish metal with their hands. Social science researchers can become equally be-clouded, as evidenced by a report suggesting that women born under certain astrological signs were more feminine than others.[15] Later efforts to replicate those studies failed to show any association between being born between July 24 and January 20 and being more womanly than other women, no matter how femininity was defined or mea-sured.[16]

These issues are sensitive; consensus on them is hard to come by. Two women generals put forth persuasive argu-ments in a recent issue of a newsmagazine on the question "Should women fight in war?" Major General Jeanne Holm of the U.S. Air Force holds that we have to get over our traditional notions about women in combat, while Brigadier General Elizabeth Hoisington of the Army says women aren't "physically, mentally, and emotionally qualified" to fight.[17]

The laws were not enacted because legislators dreamed such long dreams. They were brought about because the reality of women's situation did not jibe with our national vision of equality for all citizens. A foreign visitor, Harriet Martineau, noticed the disparity in the 1840s. American women, she wrote home, were in a restricted and depen-dent state and furthermore, "politically nonexistent." The male perspective was provided by another visitor who ob-served that woman's role here was different from man's. But he interpreted this to mean that, although her sphere was separate, it was seen as equal in importance to that of man's. Separate but equal? The phrase is suspect today and indeed

---

[15] R. J. Pellegrini, "The Astrological 'Theory' of Personality: An Un-biased Test by a Biased Observer," *Journal of Psychology*, Vol. 85 (1973), pp. 21–28.

[16] D. J. Illingworth and G. J. Syme, "Birthdate and Femininity," *Jour-nal of Social Psychology*, Vol. 103 (1977), pp. 153–154.

[17] "Pro and Con: Should Women Fight in War?" *U.S. News & World Report*, Vol. 84, No. 6 (February 13, 1978), pp. 53–54.

has been since Swedish sociologist Gunnar Myrdal undertook his massive study of the situation of black Americans. Separation had meant inequality in every realm for them. And so it has been for women.

The disparities in legal rights, educational opportunities, and—most pertinent to this analysis—employment opportunities have plagued women. Correcting these disparities is seen as unnatural by some who still accept the myths about masculinity and femininity that the new research studies challenge.

The extent to which traditionalists can act on their beliefs and preserve the conventional relationship between the sexes is severely curtailed by antidiscrimination legislation. Personnel work has been profoundly changed by the advent of these laws. Virtually every aspect of the field has been affected, including the nature of the tasks, their potential impact, and, not least of all, the division of the field into "men's jobs" and "women's jobs." The 1980s may indeed see a reversion to an earlier phase of personnel work when the needs and concerns of the individual worker were as important as the technical tasks to be accomplished. The field may be once again as open to women as to men, not because women are good at social work or not good at technical jobs but because personnel departments will take pride in choosing the most qualified candidates without regard to non-work-related factors such as sex. It is certain that the 1980s will see changes in each of the specialties in the field and no doubt the introduction of new specialties.

Personnel managers cannot rely on old beliefs about women as gospel, nor can they count on social scientists to give them the last word on sex differences. Time after time, personnel managers will find that in terms of beliefs about women otherwise sensible people still carry around a lot of baggage from the past. It is hard to get ourselves (never mind them) to put it down. It is hard too to know what to take up in its place. But the nature of personnel work requires that we commit ourselves to the effort.

Some organizations feel that they have
. . . made a "good faith" effort to
achieve goals but that negative *external* factors—such as "unavailability of
qualified candidates"—are responsible for lack of significant improvement. EEOC experience indicates that
it is far more likely that negative *internal* factors are responsible—i.e., continuing discriminatory barriers in the
employment system.

—*Federal guidebook on
affirmative action* [1]

3

Recruitment:
Casting
a Wide Net

THE Equal Employment Opportunity Commission has
looked with increasing intensity at how work organizations
recruit new workers—the procedures by which organizations let it be known that they are searching for what used to
be called "manpower." Time was when the organization
could rely on "walk-ins" to provide the major source of

[1] *Affirmative Action and Equal Employment: A Guidebook for
Employers* (Washington, D.C.: U.S. Equal Employment Opportunity
Commission, 1974), Vol. 1, p. 28.

supply for nonexempt employees; it could choose exempt employees from traditional sources, perhaps passing the word discreetly at conferences and annual meetings that the director of marketing would be retiring soon. Assistant directors of marketing in comparable companies (with younger bosses) would get the word. If a comer was spotted, the organization might carefully tailor the job description so that the requisite experience fit him—and probably only him—to the job. Now, however, the organization must prepare job descriptions and specify requisite experience and training with care and publicize its openings. In short, it must conduct a full and fair search for candidates.

The old ways, though apparently cheaper in time and money than the new procedures, were ultimately quite costly to the organization. The price? Exclusion of women (half the human race), minority men (another 7 percent), and other males in protected groups (perhaps another 10 percent, depending on the region)—theoretically, at least two-thirds of the potential applicants—from consideration for certain jobs traditionally held by white males.[2]

Changes in Recruitment

One difference between the new procedures and the old is that personnel staff members and others involved in recruiting are held accountable for their individual contributions—for their efforts toward widening a search (or narrowing it unfairly), toward requiring full and fair consideration of all (or pushing through the hiring of personal favorites). The new requirements for publicizing job openings and spelling out the requisite experience or training have changed another aspect of recruiting. New candidates themselves can make more informed decisions about whether they want to be considered for an opening. Before, when the process was shrouded in confidentiality, mana-

[2] Betty Lehan Harragan, *Games Mother Never Taught You* (New York: Rawson Associates, 1977), p. 138.

gers decided who they would encourage to apply. As a result, women who may have been quite good at a given job often had no opportunity to apply for it, because they didn't know (at the nonexempt level) that the company was hiring or (at the exempt level) that the director of marketing was retiring. Junior businesswomen used to grit their teeth with understandable frustration when they were told, "I never even *thought* of you for that job." Such comments invariably came after the fact—and typically from a manager who was telling the truth. He hadn't thought of her as a potential candidate because of long-ingrained custom.

When managers do think about why they failed to consider a woman candidate, they sometimes admit, with refreshing candor, that they carry around some of that baggage from the past. They had assumed that a woman probably would not want to "work outside," or "travel so much," or "move when her husband is here," or whatever. The obvious solution: let *her* make those decisions.

The EEOC lists six major guidelines for fair recruitment:

1. The analysis of current recruitment procedures to eliminate discriminatory barriers such as the reliance on "word of mouth" or "walk-in" sources.

2. The establishment of objective measures to monitor the recruitment process, including the development of an "applicant flow record." The aim is to be able to report on the nature of the applicant pool—that is, of all candidates, how many were females and/or minorities.

3. The training of recruiters to use only objective, job-related criteria.

4. The maintenance of files of minority and women applicants not hired for one job for use in future recruiting and the full utilization of women and minorities already on the staff as recruiters, sources of

information about potential candidates, and interviewers.

5. The publicizing of vacancies in media directed toward minorities and women by means of advertisements that include the suggested phrase "equal opportunity employer, M/F."

6. Full use of community resources, including employment services, educational institutions, minority and
women's organizations, and public training programs.[3]

The courts have ruled that reliance on walk-ins as the sole
source of new workers is discriminatory in organizations
where women and minorities are not well represented at all
levels. Which is to say: in virtually all organizations. The
guideline on maintaining applicant flow records has created
an apparent contradiction that leaves some employers
gnashing their teeth. On the one hand, they cannot ask a
prospective employee to identify herself by race in an initial interview because such a query is not work-related. On
the other hand, if the individual is not hired, the company
must report her race so as to complete flow records. If she *is*
hired, the company must note her race so as to determine
whether protected groups are being underutilized in its
workforce. It is a dilemma, clearly. But there are solutions.
An organization can ask applicants to fill out two application
forms: long and short. The long form will be the first paper
in the candidate's personal personnel record. It will contain
only questions that are job-related. The second, short form
will contain pertinent information about the candidate's
sex, race, national origin, and referral source. It will be clear
to all that this is solely for purposes of analyzing recruitment efforts and reporting on them to the government.

Why the guidelines on utilizing women and minorities
in recruitment efforts? Because the EEOC says (although in

---

[3] *Affirmative Action and Equal Employment*, Vol. 1, pp. 29–34.

more words) they work. Why the M/F tag at the end of the phrase "equal opportunity employer" in advertisements? Because, the guidelines say, "equal opportunity" is still seen to apply to racial minorities and not necessarily to women.

Some corporate officials see these guidelines as too picky, too expensive to implement, and in general too "blue sky." Some feminists, in turn, dismiss them as a typical bureaucrat's solution. ("No need to really do anything like actually *hiring* women or minorities; just do some more paperwork, and call that affirmative action.") Perhaps the most balanced view is that these modifications in the recruitment process are tiny compared with the vastness of the problem.

In the early days of the women's movement, many a woman who had problems finding work would attribute her difficulties to her age. Young women would wish they were older and older ones, younger. But as more and more women at different stages in the life cycle came together, it became clear that, for work purposes, no female could be the right age. If she was young and single, employers feared that she would get married and quit to follow her husband where his work took him. If she was married, they thought it was only a matter of time before she had babies and quit to stay home with them. If she already had children, employers thought she would be bound to stay home with them when they were sick. And if her children were too grown up to need her any longer, they thought she was over the hill.

Women in political life have been keenly aware of the outmoded notions that make their candidacy suspect to voters. An attorney was passed over for a judgeship; she was told that there was concern about her ability to both do the job and manage her family. She remarked wryly that she thought her son could handle making his own dinner. He was, at the time, 27. A candidate for a state legislature had to cope with a citizens' committee that protested her nomination on the ground that her small children needed her.

Institutions of higher education have often made it abundantly clear that they are leery of women candidates' seriousness of purpose, especially at the graduate level. A brilliant young woman was invited to be interviewed by two medical schools during the semester break of her senior year. At the first school, the interviewer asked her if she planned to be married while she was in medical school. "No," she said, "I do not. I really want to be a physician and I won't let anything interfere with that." The interviewer seemed disappointed with her answer. "We are looking for well-rounded people, you know," he said, "not just the scholar type who can't relate to human problems."

The young woman took that response under advisement, and at the interview at the second medical school, when she was asked the same question, she responded differently. "I don't honestly know," she said. "I really want to be a physician and I don't intend to let anything interfere with that. I am not in love now. But it is possible that I could fall in love while I'm still in school. And perhaps get married." The interviewer heard her out, but it was clear that he too was disappointed. "Married women are a bad risk; we know that for a fact," he said. "A bad risk." She could not help but bring home the impression that those schools didn't want her because of something that was determined before she was born: her sex.

How can business organizations keep from transmitting such messages to prospective women employees? Perhaps the first step is to consider, as the EEOC suggests, the inequities that can arise under traditional recruitment practices.

How Job Openings Were Made Known in the Past

Research studies suggest strongly that most people find jobs through word of mouth. Somebody they know knows somebody who in turn knows about an opening. Many a blue collar girl has found her factory job because one of her relatives heard the company was hiring and mentioned it to her family. Professional-level openings have likewise been filled by passing the word of opportunities through the network of colleagues. In academic life, a department chairman would phone his colleagues at other institutions to ask if they had "any good men coming along."

Dr. Lilli Hornig, director of the Higher Education Resource Services, a nonprofit agency that seeks to match academic candidates with appropriate posts in higher education, reports that in her opinion this was not necessarily a conspiracy to keep women out. It was just that the men didn't think of their women graduate students as aspiring to jobs at the same level as the men or as needing placement at all. Another factor, according to Hornig, is that male faculty tend to undervalue the achievements of women students, regardless of their records. Women candidates may be passed over for other reasons. The chairman may be hesitant about introducing conflict into a married woman's life by considering her for a job far from her husband's work site. The chairman may assume that she wouldn't leave him and he wouldn't follow her. Why pursue it? A woman candidate may have taken time out after earning a degree. The chairman may assume that she is out of the job market for an extended period. In any case, once she is out of the communications network, she no longer gets word of an opportunity that might bring her back to work.

Professional women face a particularly difficult problem in fields where important contacts are made at the annual professional meetings. A senior manager may invite a promising male assistant to go with him and take pride in introducing his protégé to his colleagues. He may hesitate to do the same for an equally promising woman assistant for fear that their relationship will be misunderstood.

No law can be enacted to solve some of these problems. But there are steps a company can take to insure that it is casting a sufficiently wide net to attract candidates who previously might not have thought of applying. Widening the net—indeed, making any modification in recruitment practices—may be seen as controversial. Personnel managers may be criticized from outside the company: few aspects of the work are more public than recruitment activities. They may encounter resistance from within as well.

A busy line manager may phone personnel some afternoon with the word that at last his department has permission to "hire another gal." "We're really jammed up over here," he explains. "My 'girl' is out sick. Even when she's here, there is too much for her to handle." He wants the new employee to start as soon as possible, even tomorrow. Sometimes he mentions somebody who would be right for the job; other times he may make a half-joking comment that what the department really needs is a "cute, blonde chick to brighten things up around here." He may describe some movie star or TV personality and say, "Send me one like her."

At this juncture, the personnel representative has the unenviable task of transmitting the following news: no permanent employee can be hired overnight. A job description must be prepared, the post has to be classified by pay range and level, the opening itself must be advertised. Depending on company policy, the opening may be made known to those on staff some days before it is made public. The company may have a policy of giving consideration first to those on layoff status, next to those currently employed who may seek lateral transfers or advancement, and finally to others.

The personnel manager may be well advised to tell the caller that the job advertisement cannot express a preference by sex, race, or age. No matter how high the caller's motives, he cannot reserve any job (clerical post or vice presidency) for a woman. The line manager may fume at the red tape and resulting delays involved. It is even more likely that he will take umbrage at the implication that by his joking remark he was discriminating against anybody. Accusing any worker (no matter how indirectly) of being racist is, as a rule, inflammatory.

Comments suggesting that managers are being sexist

are, in contrast, sometimes received as compliments. More than one personnel manager has had to endure being told in braggardly and patronizing tones that the caller is indeed a male chauvinist and proud of it. If the opening is technical, the caller may inform personnel that everybody knows there are no women with that training. If the position is in management—in a range of jobs that have been defined as "one step away from the work"—the caller may well betray the fact that he has never even considered the possibility that such a job could be done by a woman.

The Full and Fair Search

Where employers look for applicants may well determine who they find. Perhaps the single most useful service an equal opportunity officer can provide is up-to-date lists of women's job rosters, women's caucuses within the professional associations in each discipline, and women's organizations. The personnel officer will use discretion in choosing among the resources. One EEO officer advised a search committee to advertise an opening for a staff attorney in *Woman's Day* so as to be sure to attract well-qualified women. Such counsel, though well intentioned, is not useful. But there are publications (seldom those with recipes) in each field that may reach the very candidates the company hopes to attract.

Employers who have traditionally recruited on campus must be particularly sensitive to which colleges they choose to visit. The single-sex institution is less favored today by parents and high school graduates, but many distinguished women's colleges still take pride in preparing women to serve as leaders in society. Similarly, the predominantly black colleges may prove to be good sources of talent. Recruiters who visit coeducational institutions must remember to be as open to women candidates as to men. A major law school was the scene of controversy two years ago when one firm sent a recruiter who objected to having to interview women. His rationale was that although he personally had no objection to seeing women applicants, he was certain that the partners would continue to hire only males and that he would therefore be wasting the women's time. Some of the men in that graduating class were not prepared to be interviewed by a firm with such policies. That recruiter's schedule was full of holes during his days on campus. Many observers felt that it was a brave action on the part of the men at a time when jobs for attorneys were difficult to find—or at least more difficult than they had been.

Recruiters need to be careful to avoid illegal pre-employment inquiries. Married women candidates report that they often have the curious feeling their husbands are being interviewed at one remove when the recruiter raises certain questions ("How does your husband feel about the work you do?" "How would he feel about moving?" "Doesn't he get upset when dinner is late?"). Another problem, commonly reported on white college campuses, is the excessive zeal with which women and minority candidates are welcomed. Recruiters can make offensive and needlessly effusive comments about how very happy they are to have "an affirmative action candidate." [4] Such comments may make candidates feel that they are welcome solely because of sex or race, without regard to qualifications.

Perhaps the safest posture for the interviewer is a matter-of-fact approach to each candidate. The very presence of a recruiter at a women's college or predominantly black institution signifies interest in interviewing candidates there. It may be unnecessary to reiterate a commitment to equal opportunity. Similarly, the recruiter should refrain from treating the woman engineer or minority candidate in business administration differently from the white male candidates interviewed there traditionally. Thus *where* a company recruits can be influential in the later appraisal of whether the search was truly full and fair.

---

[4] Charles W. Marks, "Is Your Bias Showing?" *Personnel Journal,* Vol. 57, No. 8 (August 1977), p. 381.

Equally important is the way the opening is described in advertising and by word of mouth. Psychologist Sandra Bem's experiments suggest strongly that the way an employer describes a job may have an important influence on the sex composition of the applicants who respond. Those who compose advertisements should take pains to make sure that the statement at the bottom ("This organization is an equal opportunity employer") is not undermined by the wording of the advertisement itself. Repeated reference to "*his* qualifications," "*he* will be expected," "benefits available to *him*" may negate the effect of the EEO commitment by transmitting a preference for males. Of course, companies boycott publications that still have separate "Help Wanted—Female" and "Help Wanted—Male" columns. *How* an employer advertises an opening is, therefore, as influential in some respects as where.

The crucial question of timing has proven to be a stumbling block for employers. By the time the members of the search committee or the line manager and personnel come to agreement on the way the job opening will be described, there may be little time available for the search. But the job must be publicized for a fair length of time: *when* recruiting begins and ends is important. One cannot expect management consultants, employment agencies, or job rosters to marshal a phalanx of women candidates overnight. A job description written in haste can put unnecessary restraints on a search. Does the job truly require a college graduate? Supposing a candidate of either sex appears who is well qualified by virtue of experience. Then the manager may wish he had left himself some flexibility.

Justice for Internal Candidates

The problem faced by women, as was suggested in Chapter 1, is not their lack of jobs but the kinds of jobs they hold. Thus the issue is not so much how to encourage housewives to come to work as how to encourage interest in advancement among qualified women already in the company. A representative of the National Association of Manufacturers opines that it is easier, really, for companies to meet their EEO goals by hiring from outside. In fact, a comparison of corporate advances in recruiting versus training their own to assume positions of more responsibility suggests that whether it is easier or not, companies are doing better with recruiting. There are exceptions. AT&T, the largest employer of women in the United States, has instituted an assessment center to aid in identifying potential among its employees, both women and men. Follow-up studies suggest that the center works as well for women of all races and minority men as it does for white men.

The Ford Motor Company has inaugurated a computer-assisted retrieval system for identifying women and minorities already in its employ who have skills that might be suited to job openings at a higher level. A third method, used more commonly, is for supervisors to evaluate each staff member's performance every year. In a counseling session, the supervisor discusses the written performance evaluation with the worker, who in turn has an opportunity to comment if he or she chooses. These evaluations are filed in personnel, where they can be utilized as an informal skills bank. The weakness of this method, like other techniques used to identify staff members who are suited for the "fast track," is that it relies on the competence and unselfishness of the supervisor. He must evaluate his secretary objectively even as he knows that, should he rave, he may soon lose her.

A representative of a major life insurance company reports that her organization is absolutely sincere in its wish to do wide recruiting. In fact, she says, a test developed by the company has proved to be quite accurate in assessing the skills and aptitudes that predict, for white males, success as an insurance salesworker. The test has been validated for women as well, but too few minorities have taken it to establish its validity for that group. (Before a test is deemed fair for a group, members of the group take it for validation purposes but are not judged by the results; the applicant's record merely shows that the test was taken.) Selling insurance is a high-pressure job; the turnover rate is high. Of 100 hired this year, only 12 or 14 will still be with the company in four years. As a result, she says, the company would vacuum people in off the street to take the test if it could.

Her company may be overlooking a potential source of talent close at hand: its own clerical workforce. Since the education requirements for selling insurance are flexible (successful agents include those with MBAs, college graduates, college dropouts, and high school dropouts), it might be the case that some of the women clerks, typists, secretaries, and stenographers are suited to selling. The company's representative feels that few clerical workers would try for the job. Internal posting of openings would be a way to test the hypothesis.

A study of university employees undertaken in 1972 uncovered a source of friction among the clerical workers. Women from the community reported that they felt the institution favored spouses of students in hiring and in advancement. Employees related to students, in contrast, reported having been told that they were considered transients and less satisfactory overall than permanent residents. So it is with external versus internal candidates. Those from outside, ascertaining that internal candidates already familiar with the organization, feel themselves to be at a disadvantage. Internal candidates or prospective candidates are certain that they are looked at through different glasses and evaluated less favorably. External candidates' strengths, they feel, are always more apparent than their weaknesses. In this case, the would-be candidates already on the scene are probably correct.

Women in magazine publishing, traditionally channeled into research and support jobs, press for opportunities to try for writer-reporter jobs. They are told that there are no openings. Before the advent of job posting, many found that when an opening did develop, the news did not make its way to them in time to apply. In fact, the first they knew of any writing job open was the day a new writer reported for work, having been hired the week before.[5]

A research organization found itself in trouble when it did not really search within its own ranks before hiring. A woman already there got word that a new position had been authorized, and she believed herself to be well suited for it. Submitting her credentials, she was invited to make a presentation to the department heads, which she was fully prepared to do. Several days before her scheduled presentation, a male candidate was brought in to give his. She and the other members of the staff were invited, as was customary, to hear him. She did. After the seminar, she heard members of the search committee offering to help him look for a house. The clear implication was that he was essentially hired; her presentation would be a formality. This grievance was not easy to resolve; all the satisfaction she got, after lengthy hearings, was an apology and a promise that such a thing would not happen again.

Managers are well advised to treat the internal candidate just as they would external candidates. If outside candidates have individual interviews with department members or heads of units, so should she. If it is customary to take outside candidates to lunch, she should be accorded that courtesy. As others submit sets of credentials for review, so should she. Whether she should be invited to hear other candidates' presentations may have to be decided with some care. Is she being deprived in her role as department member by not being invited? Is she being given unfair advantage over other candidates because she cn hear their presentations? One compromise would be to invite her to give hers first.

[5] Ethel Strainchamps (ed.), *Rooms with No View: A Woman's Guide to the Man's World of the Media* (New York: Harper & Row, 1974), pp. 27–92.

The Spurious Ad

One problem that causes bad feeling among women candidates and among men who are rejected is the suspicion that the hiring decision was made long before the job was posted. To comply with the requirement that a search be full and fair, those in charge of hiring, it is feared, go through the motions of bringing in women and/or minorities to be interviewed. But everyone knows, from the start, that the job is essentially filled. Such claims are hard to prove—unless somebody is indiscreet enough to allude to helping one candidate find a house in another candidate's hearing, to be sure. No matter how open managers may be and how truly undecided they are when candidates are being interviewed, those who lose out may be suspicious that the hire was a foregone conclusion. Perhaps the most difficult (and unnecessary) problem arises when a search *is* fair and white males who are turned away are told that preference is being given to minorities or to females. This is particularly galling to all concerned when the white male goes away embittered by what he terms a case of reverse discrimination. And a white male is hired in the end.

The moral of that sad story is that personnel practitioners should counsel managers to be exceedingly careful during the recruitment process, especially in the reasons they give or imply for an individual applicant's rejection.

In the course of casting a wide net, companies are well advised to be as innovative as AT&T in establishing an assessment center and to be as flexible as the insurance company in not requiring certain credentials but concentrating instead on the potential to do the job. The vice president of a New York bank has expanded his recruiting program to include not only the traditional career fairs at high schools and the usual interviews on business school campuses but meetings with women's organizations as well. There, he encourages older women who may be contemplating reentry to consider the range of occupations open to them in banks. A drug company in Westchester County serves that community by permitting women to use its corporate lounges and auditorium for meetings of career cooperatives—groups of older women who get together to share information about job openings, techniques for finding professional-level work, and avenues for updating their training.

Employers who word their advertising to suggest that they are flexible about credentials (for example, "bachelor's degree *or equivalent*") may tap into a rich lode of women of all ages who could be excellent additions to the staff. A crack in the armor of rigidity that seems to surround some companies appeared during the last recruiting season on a university campus. Recruiters from a large Midwestern company were meeting with MBA candidates, as was their custom. They were perhaps a little surprised when an undergraduate, a social work major, appeared. She had been dissatisfied with the range of openings posted in her department so she decided to seek an interview at the graduate student level. The recruiters talked with her and indeed hired her for their management training program.

It is clear that some women are taking fullest advantage of every opportunity open to them—and are creating opportunities where none appear to exist—but many are still losing out. Girls outnumber boys in high school graduating classes. Indeed, girls earn higher grades in high school than boys but are less likely to go on to college.[6] A research study conducted by the Carnegie Foundation showed that the greatest loss of talent in our country is among blue collar girls who score high on SATs but do not go to college. This trend may soon be changed. According to the National Center for Education Statistics, the number of students enrolling in college in 1977 was up 366,541 from 1976.

[6] Ruth B. Cowan, "Legal Barriers to Social Change: The Case of Higher Education," in the Equal Rights Amendment Project, California Commission on the Status of Women (eds.), *Impact ERA: Limitations and Possibilities* (Millbrae, Cal.: Les Femmes, 1976), pp. 158–183.

Women comprised no less than 93 percent of that enrollment growth.[7]

An important question regarding recruitment is: Who does it? In some companies, only the trained interviewers from personnel have that responsibility. In others, virtually every salesperson is encouraged to keep an eye out for likely recruits, including women and minorities. The latter policy has the advantage of widening the search, but it also increases the possibility that someone will represent the company badly, albeit unwittingly. Knowing the difference between asking "Do you speak Spanish?" (a legitimate request for information) and "How come you know Spanish so well?" (a questionable inquiry) is not something an employee learns overnight. There is risk of offending potential recruits and of breaking the law in questioning women about how they will manage full-time work and the responsibility of little children. Questions to women about children's health, babysitting arrangements, or birth control invade privacy and furthermore are illegal unless the same questions are asked of comparable male applicants.

The preemployment interview and indeed the whole recruitment effort is fraught with ambiguity. Some institutions seek to transmit as much information as possible in advertising their job openings by marking some "strong internal candidate." This raises more questions than it answers. Is there another category? That is, do some advertisements carry the notation "internal candidate," meaning no competition from that quarter? Is there any sense in applying, as an outsider, when such a phrase is included? The best counsel to job applicants is to apply if they believe themselves to be qualified.

Even the best-intentioned efforts are not always crowned with success. One manager carefully advertised his openings in *The New York Times*. Next day, he got an

<hr/>

[7] Jack Magarrell, "Women Account for 93 Percent of Enrollment Gain," *Chronicle of Higher Education*, Vol. 15, No. 17 (January 9, 1978), pp. I and II.

irate phone call from the editor of a newspaper that served the black community. Apologizing for not having thought to advertise there, the manager concealed the fact that he had not even heard of the paper the caller represented. He promised to consider advertising there as well. And he would have, except that he talked with one of his co-workers who had gotten a similar call from an editor who represented a paper serving the Puerto Rican community. Next day, they both got calls from an editor whose paper was aimed at another ethnic group. And the voice was familiar.

The managers phoned their EEO officer, who advised them to forget advertising in papers like that. They are mimeographed handouts, with a tiny circulation—all distributed by the same man. So much for widely known, widely circulated papers that no EEO officer has ever heard of.

The sense of injustice nursed by some majority men blooms in full flower when they fall prey to a sharp operator who somehow cons them into buying advertising in a nonexistent directory that, they are told on the phone, will reach minority audiences. Somehow their anger at being ripped off is directed at the black community or at women, when indeed the perpetrators of these fraudulent operations are, according to *Washington Post* reports, white men. It is fair to be outraged at this fraud, which is said to be costing corporations $25 million a year,[8] but it is clearly not fair to blame government or minorities for management naiveté.

Applicants often hear (or think they hear) outrageous comments and questions in interviews. Sometimes they have completely misunderstood what was going on. One young woman came away from one of her first interviews certain that she would receive an offer. When she was rejected, she couldn't believe it. "He asked me if I was plan-

---

[8] Lou Cannon, "Business Directory Fraud Preys on 'White Guilt,' " *Ithaca (N.Y.) Journal*, Inside Supplement, January 21, 1978, p. 3. Reprinted from the *Washington Post*.

ning to get married," she said. "I knew that was a test to see
if I know the law about what kinds of questions you can ask.
I figured he was also looking to see if I was a real feminist
and not just a person who brags about being one. So of
course I called him on the question and I really showed him
that I wasn't one of your smiling shrinking-violet types."

Only after some reflection and additional experience in
other interviews did she realize that she had read that first
one entirely wrong. She had made two fundamental mis-
takes. First, she had misinterpreted the question. Fact is,
the interviewer wanted to know how long the company
could count on her—which is precisely what he should
have asked. Second, she was in error in thinking that he
knew or cared about her commitment to feminism. He was
seeking a good employee who wanted to work for the company, who was willing to learn to do things its way, and who
showed the kind of initiative that might lead to innovation
someday. Just not tomorrow.

Misunderstandings in interviews may continue to come
about. Some will lead to loss of employees the company
wouldn't have wanted anyway. Others will leave the inter-
viewee hoping she or he will be invited back to learn more
about what's going on. And other interviews will lead to the
courts.

But the institution of wider searches and more publicity
in recruiting is surely to the advantage of management,
applicant, and employee. For many years, academic vacancies in England have been posted for the benefit of all concerned. When such an idea was introduced in the United
States, serious objections were raised by academics. Some
professors felt very strongly that it was undignified to place
a "help wanted" ad for a scholar. Others conceded that it
might be all right and even useful to advertise in the professional journals, where readers would more likely be qualified, but absolutely idiotic to publish an ad in the local
newspaper. "There is nobody in this town qualified for this
appointment," they'd say. "If there were, I'd know her."

Others were not so certain that the town was devoid of

qualified newcomers or of people who know people elsewhere. In any case, the policy was instituted. One professor complained that he had cast his net so wide that it broke. He had to buy new file cabinets to accommodate the hundreds of letters of inquiry and résumés and recommendations and vitas that flooded in. As the tidal wave of mail increased, he began to realize that his advertisement had been amateurish. He had neglected to specify the specialty he wanted; he had forgotten to indicate a closing date for responses, and he hadn't put in enough information about the job level. The mail increased; he barely had time to open the envelopes. At least he did get permission to hire a clerical worker to help put the letters in order and address form letters of response to applicants.

He picked up the telephone to call personnel. "We are really jammed up over here," he began. At that moment, an attractive young blonde walked past his office door and clucked sympathetically at the sight of the piles of unopened mail. He described her to personnel and said he wanted one like her. Fast! And you know what personnel responded.

> When [young Florence Cohen] arrived for the interview and gave her name, she was told at once that the firm never employed Jews. "No," said the interviewer, "Jews are not ever permitted to work here. They are all troublemakers."
>
> —*Dana Gross Schecter, describing an incident in 1912* [1]

4

Selection: Choosing the Best

ACCORDING to the Equal Employment Opportunity Commission, experience under Title VII indicates that the selection process is probably responsible for more discrimination than any other area of employment practice. Long before Florence Cohen went to apply for work as a typist (and long since), some employers have been using non-work-related criteria to make selection decisions.

---

[1] Interview of Florence Cohen Gross by Dana Gross Schecter, November 14, 1975, quoted in Barbara Mayer Wertheimer, *We Were There: The Story of Working Women in America* (New York: Pantheon Books, 1977), p. 234.

The EEOC has, accordingly, set up guidelines to assist employers. These can be summarized as follows:

1. Selection procedures must be based on job-related standards. In other words, any criteria a manager chooses to use—from candidates' experience or education to performance on any preemployment test—must be demonstrably related to job performance.
2. If affected classes appear to be discriminated against by the criteria chosen, the employer must be able to show that its hiring standards are valid in that they do indeed differentiate between people who can do the specific job and candidates who cannot.[2]

The EEOC notes that non-job-related educational requirements that have disparate effect on protected groups constitute a major area of illegal discrimination. For example, a requirement that candidates for a custodial position have high school diplomas serves to disqualify minorities at a higher rate than others. Such a requirement is valid only if the employer can demonstrate that completion of high school is directly related to performance as a custodian in the company. An example from the professional level? Although none is provided by the EEOC, this example seems parallel: the requirement that an attorney have experience practicing on Wall Street to be qualified for service as employee relations counsel. If this serves to disqualify women and/or minority attorneys at a disparate rate (and it certainly does, since only white male attorneys were partners in Wall Street firms for many years), the burden of proof is on the employer to demonstrate that such experience is directly related to performance as an employee relations counsel for the firm.

At the Boston Symphony Orchestra, auditions for new

[2] *Affirmative Action and Equal Employment: A Guidebook for Employers* (Washington, D.C.: U.S. Equal Employment Opportunity Commission, 1974), Vol. 1, pp. 35–40.

members focus solely on the candidate's ability to do the job. The judges sit on one side of a screen; the applicant enters the room on the other side and, unseen by them, sits down and plays. The judges decide, solely on the basis of what they hear, who will make the "short list" of applicants. This can result in teachers being cut before their pupils; it can bring about a considerable imbalance in the age of applicants on the short list. But the orchestra is committed to auditioning just that way. Indeed, applicants are cautioned to take off their shoes before they enter the room so that the judges will not be influenced by hearing a step that sounds masculine or feminine, aged or youthful.

If managers advertise far and wide and then select candidates for interviews solely on the basis of performance, they will be in compliance with both the letter and the spirit of the equal employment opportunity legislation. Most employers find, however, that their criteria are harder to validate than those of the Boston Symphony. Presumably, it is possible for judges to come to agreement about the quality of performance they hear from behind a screen. But supposing managers have other criteria—such as ability to work with a group—for selection in another line of work? Problems can arise if the standards they use to sort out applicants have a disparate effect on women and minorities unless those standards can be shown to be associated with performance on the job.

To what extent is an employer allowed to take the sex and race composition of its workforce into account in staffing? This question is not entirely resolved in American courts. In Sweden, questions of admissions quotas are not so controversial as they are in the United States. At one college, a number of places in every class are set aside for members of a minority group. Presumably there are times when the credentials of majority applicants are better than those of the minorities, with the result that a majority candidate with (say) high grades on admissions tests will be rejected while a minority candidate with lower grades will be admitted. The issue is not seen as controversial, because the admissions policies were designed to help the country reach a national goal. What is interesting is the goal that takes precedence over admissions based solely on individual merit. The college in Sweden trains people to administer and staff child care centers. Swedes put a high priority on integrating men into the occupation.

In the United States, if women and minorities are underrepresented in their organizations in the posts they are seeking to fill, employers are well advised to scrutinize their standards with special care. If it develops that they are indeed using discriminatory criteria or if a pattern of underutilization can be demonstrated, employers may be required to move toward a quota system such as the one described above. Consent decrees will spell out in detail what proportion of each new group of hires must be women and/or minorities. The consent decree signed by Brown University requires that until there is "full utilization of women faculty based on statistical availability," the university shall "apply affirmative action on behalf of women faculty . . . by giving preference to a female candidate of equal qualifications over nonminority males." [3] Comparable consent decrees have been signed by construction companies, by steel companies, and, as noted earlier, by AT&T.

How can personnel practitioners assist line managers in making selection decisions that will not be challenged in court and that will be as objective as humanly possible? Perhaps the first step is for practitioners to become acquainted with the biases that can enter into selection decisions. We shall consider three types: the bias that seems to be present in the heads of women themselves, the bias that may be affecting others' assessment of women, and the bias that is built into the system. Management may be continuing some practices which, although neutral on the surface, do in fact result in unfair and illegal discrimination.

[3] U.S. District Court for the District of Rhode Island, Louise Lamphere . . . v. Brown University, C.A. 75-0140, p. 1.

Problems in Women's Heads

As was noted earlier, women who retire from the work-force for a period of time to care for their children often suffer from a "collapse of confidence" that cripples them in searching for a job. A classic example came about when a company advertised for a computer programmer. The first people to respond to the ad were a middle-aged woman and a 19-year-old man, a freshman at a nearby college.

In the interview, the woman asked hesitantly what language the programmers would be expected to use. "I only know Fortran," she said apologetically. "And I'm rusty on that. It has been six months since I used it. I'm not sure I can get my speed back up right away—not sure at all."

And the man? Upon hearing the requirements of the job, he said, "Sure, I can do computer programming, I'm sure I can. I read a book on it once."

He got the job.

Virginia Radley, the first woman to serve as president of an academic unit of the State University of New York, has commented that there does seem to be a difference in the way males and females evaluate their own capabilities. For a high-level position, an employer may list ten qualifications. A man is likely to apply even if he lacks up to half the qualifications by an objective standard; a woman won't submit her application if she lacks even one.

A woman professor of engineering at the Massachusetts Institute of Technology offers another example of observed differences between the sexes. She notes that the members of an entering class often do not do well on their first tests of the term. The men look at their returned papers in disbelief and tend to blame the professor, saying, "What a terrible test! Unfair!" Women, in contrast, receive the news equally sadly but seem to react by asking, "Do I really belong in engineering?"

In a recent review of the literature, Terborg found that women as a group "describe themselves and are described by men as having self-concepts that are not suitable for management [posts]." [4] This does not seem to be a reflection of reality. The Human Engineering Laboratory has isolated 22 abilities that are linked with managerial success. After evaluating thousands of tests administered to males and females, laboratory staff members assert with confidence that males and females do not differ in the extent to which they possess 14 of these traits. Males do excel on two of the dimensions; but females excel on six.[5] Despite what women may think, they as a group are more suited to holding management posts than men are.

But here, as elsewhere, self-confidence is vital. It has been noted that, for a high school girl, being pretty is an important factor. Indeed, it does not appear to matter whether she is or not. What she thinks is the pertinent reality. If she doesn't think she is pretty, she may as well not be.

Problems in the Heads of Others

Self-appraisal and appraisal by others are of course closely related. Cooley's phrase "the looking-glass self" captures the interrelatedness well. We are what we see reflected in the eyes of others. Some individuals are more independent than others and less reliant on other people's judgments, but no man (or woman) is an island. Bardwick and others have noted a striking difference between the sexes: girls are reared to be more responsive to signals from others than boys are and thus develop more sensitivity to others' judgments than their brothers do.

A psychology professor has noted that we are often unaware of how others influence us. He learned this, he relates, by experience. Unknown to him, his graduate stu-

---

[4] James R. Terborg, "Women in Management: A Research Review," *Journal of Applied Psychology*, Vol. 62, No. 6 (December 1977), pp. 647–664, p. 658.

[5] Elizabeth B. Bolton and Luther Wade Humphreys, "A Training Model for Women: An Androgynous Approach," *Personnel Journal*, Vol. 56, No. 5 (May 1977), pp. 230–234.

dents decided that he spent too much time behind the podium when he gave a lecture. In collusion with the other students in that large lecture class, they set about to test the hypothesis that they could change the professor's behavior without his realizing it. For some weeks that term, the students practiced what they had learned in his text: that positive reinforcement changes behavior. Whenever he stepped from behind the podium, they would look interested, smile, and nod intelligently. When he returned to the podium, they would look down at their notebooks or permit their eyes to glaze over with boredom.

By his own report, it was a happy term for the professor. He came to think of himself as a really effective teacher, even a comedian. The students were so responsive, so interested, so ready to react with enthusiasm! Only then did his graduate students show him the chart of "time away from podium." It demonstrated how, without his knowing it, they had increased that time substantially over the term.

Perhaps the most hopeful study of behavior change was undertaken by a psychologist in an elementary school. At the beginning of the term, he tested all the students in one teacher's class and reported to her privately that certain ones (whom he identified by name) showed great potential. At the end of the term, he retested the class and found that students in the experimental group did in fact perform better on the test; they also earned better grades in all their subjects than their classmates not singled out. The ones he identified to the teacher at first had been chosen at random. We can conclude that there was something in the interaction between the teacher and the students she believed to have the greatest potential that caused those students to perform up to her expectations. This is known as the "Rosenthal effect." It may well be related to the effect observed at the Hawthorne plant, reported in Chapter 1. Both the Rosenthal effect and the Hawthorne effect show how much social expectations influence behavior.

There are less encouraging findings on the appraisal of women's performance at work by both men and women.

Laboratory studies have shown that the same research papers are rated higher when they are thought to be written by men than when they are believed to be written by women.[6] A related experiment was undertaken with identical works of art signed with male names for some subjects and with female names for others. Those thought to be executed by females were judged less favorably than those purportedly done by males. A variation of this experiment did prove to reduce the bias: if the subjects believed that the artwork had won a prize, the male/female difference in evaluation disappeared.

Women's success is, according to psychologist Kay Deaux, often attributed to luck, while men's is thought to be due to individual talent.[7] Cline has shown that intellectual products are judged more favorably when they are thought to be men's than women's; she adds this sobering note: we all may be sex chauvinists. Women tend to favor women's efforts over men's, while men favor men's efforts over women's.[8]

Mohr and Downey, in turn, have cast doubt on the objectivity of "peer ratings" among military officers. Men and women rated themselves and others on performance radically differently. The authors suggest that they might be using different criteria for the males, who would have different assignments (for example, combat versus support work) after training.[9]

What are the implications of these findings for improving selection procedures? It does appear that we may not be able to trust ourselves to judge people's credentials fairly when we know their sex. As Schein suggests, when we

[6] Phillip Goldberg, "Are Women Prejudiced Against Women?" *Transaction*, Vol. 5, No. 5 (April 1968), pp. 28–30.

[7] Kay Deaux, *The Behavior of Women and Men* (Belmont, Cal.: Wadsworth, 1976).

[8] Mary Ellen Cline et al., "Evaluations of the Work of Men and Women as a Function of the Sex of the Judge and Type of Work," *Journal of Applied Social Psychology*, Vol. 7, No. 1 (January–March 1977), pp. 89–93.

[9] E. Sue Mohr and Ronald G. Downey, "Are Women Peers?" *Journal of Occupational Psychology*, Vol. 50, No. 1 (March 1977), pp. 53–57.

think of filling a manager's job, we may all automatically "think male." [10] This may be the case even when we have "objective" test results to help inform our decisions. Heneman reports that high-scoring females were still ranked as less suitable for insurance saleswork than males who scored lower.[11]

Problems in the System

A number of institutional customs, practices, and policies appear to be neutral but nevertheless have differential impact on the sexes. An instructive example comes from a university. A 1972 study showed that occupational groups at Cornell University were clearly differentiated by sex.[12] Table 3 shows the sex imbalance. It can be seen that women, who make up half the workforce of nearly 7,000 people, hold only 10 percent of the faculty posts and 85 percent of the clerical jobs. Cornell is not unique in this; the institution studied by Ferber and Westmiller is quite similar, as are many others.[13]

Much of the disparity in the Cornell study can be traced to the women's level of education. A person of either sex with a high school diploma or a bachelor's degree seldom holds a professorship. As a control on educational level, data were gathered on the 430 university employees with master's degrees. A comparison of the posts held by these men and women is given in Table 4. The data show that 96

[10] Virginia E. Schein, "Think Manager—Think Male," *Atlanta Economic Review*, Vol. 26, No. 2 (March–April 1976), pp. 21–24.

[11] Herbert G. Heneman, "The Impact of Test Information and Applicant Sex on Applicant Evaluations in a Selection Simulation," *Journal of Applied Psychology*, Vol. 62, No. 4 (August 1977), pp. 524–526.

[12] Jennie Farley, "Men, Women, and Work Satisfaction on Campus," *Cornell Journal of Social Relations*, Vol. 9, No. 1 (Spring 1974), pp. 87–97. (Available as Reprint 366, New York State School of Industrial and Labor Relations, Cornell University, Ithaca, N.Y. 14853.)

[13] Marianne A. Ferber and Anne Westmiller, "Sex and Race Differences in Nonacademic Wages on a University Campus," *Journal of Human Resources*, Vol. 11, No. 3 (Summer 1976), pp. 366–373.

Table 3. Cornell University employees (N = 3,962), by job category and sex, 1972.

Job Category	Percent Female
Faculty (professor, associate professor, assistant professor)	10
Parafaculty (instructor, lecturer, research associate)	34
Senior staff (university officer, dean, director)	10
Junior staff (professionals: accountant to writer)	38
Research staff (research specialist, research technician)	34
Librarians (people with professional library training)	73
Supervisors (superintendent, foreman, supervisor)	31
White collar (people in clerical work, sales)	85
Blue collar (service workers, all others)	36

percent of the men with master's degrees hold professional jobs (from supervisor to faculty member), while only 77 percent of the women with equivalent education do; 7 percent of the women (14 individuals) have faculty posts, while 31 percent of the men (73 individuals) are on the faculty.

What kinds of posts do women with Master's degrees have? About a fifth are classified as "parafaculty" or "white collar" respectively; a quarter are professional librarians. Tables 5, 6, and 7 show the position of women in each of these groups. The data make it clear that women are bunched at the bottom of each career ladder. They are less likely to be instructors than their male colleagues and less likely to have climbed from administrative aide to administrative assistant; they are absolutely absent from the ranks of those who direct the libraries. The higher the job level, the fewer the women.

Table 4. Cornell employees holding master's degrees, by sex and job category, 1972.

Job Level	Master's Holders	
	Males (N = 234)	Females (N = 196)
Faculty	31%	7%
Parafaculty	21	21
Senior staff	10	2
Junior staff	15	7
Research staff	7	11
Librarians	9	25
Supervisors	3	4
White collar	3	21
Blue collar	1	2
	100%	100%

Table 5. Parafaculty posts at Cornell University, Ithaca campus, by sex and rank, 1972.

Title	Total Number	Number Women	Percent Women
Visiting professor	51	6	12
Teaching associate	2	—	—
Visiting lecturer	43	3	7
Instructor [a]	88	22	25
Lecturer [b]	100	58	58
Postdoctoral fellow	88	11	13
Research associate	222	40	18
Extension associate [d]	44	22	50
	638	162	25 [c]

Source: Cornell University Directory, 1971–1972.
[a] A post considered, in some units, as a ladder step (a job that leads to an assistant professorship and thus to consideration for tenure). Of the 22 women holding instructorships, however, 11 are in the department of physical education, where the posts are nonladder, since there are no faculty in physical education.
[b] A unique category in that virtually all the posts are part-time jobs.
[c] Average, all positions.
[d] A post (unique to land grant institutions) which involves extending what is being studied and taught at universities to wider audiences, i.e., the job of adult education professional.

Table 6. Administrative assistants and administrative aides, Cornell University, by sex and rank, 1972.

Title	Total Number	Number Women	Percent Women
Administrative assistant 4	2	—	—
Administrative assistant 3	6	1	17
Administrative assistant 2	26	9	35
Administrative assistant 1	27	11	41
Administrative aide 2	43	40	93
Administrative aide 1	86	83	97
	190	144	76*

Source: Cornell University Senate Constituency List, January 1972.
* Average, all positions.

Table 7. Professional librarians, Cornell University, by sex and rank, 1972.

Title	Total Number	Number Women	Percent Women
Director	1	—	—
Associate director	2	—	—
Assistant director	2	—	—
Professor	1	—	—
Instructor	1	—	—
Bibliographer	2	—	—
Librarian	23	15	65
Associate librarian	27	18	66
Senior assistant librarian	16	13	81
Assistant librarian	39	26	67
	114	72	63*

Source: Cornell University Senate Constituency List, January 1972.
* Average, all positions.

This university, like others, appears to be "underutilizing" women's talents. Some of the reasons for the imbalance are outside the control of the institution, to be sure. The question is, however: To what extent can the university be held culpable?

Cornell has drawn national attention as a leader in the

education of women. Its founders were committed to offering opportunities to students of both sexes; it was one of the
first institutions in the country to admit women more than
100 years ago; it is high on the list of undergraduate institutions whose women graduates go on to earn the Ph.D.[14]
Even as recently as 1950, Cornell was the only institution in
the Ivy League that admitted women on an equal basis with
men—that is, not into a coordinate women's college or into
a special women's curriculum.

Recent evidence gathered by Charlotte Conable
suggests, however, that a bias was built into the system as
early as 1900. The university's housing policy had a demon-
strable effect on the number of women admitted and on the
subjects they studied. It was felt that women needed more
supervision and protection than men did. As a result,
women (but not men) were required to live in university
dormitories. The limited number of beds in the women's
dormitories were allocated to each college within the university in proportion to the number of women students in
that college. Few women applied to engineering; few were
accepted there. Therefore, few beds in the dormitory were
allocated to engineering for women for the following
year—and ever after. Soon the bed quota began to determine the admissions quota. In that way, women were artifi-
cially restricted to certain fields: the liberal arts and home
economics. Since there had once been few women in the
"masculine" fields of engineering, veterinary medicine, ag-
riculture, architecture, industrial and labor relations, and
hotel administration, the underrepresentation of women
there was perpetuated.[15]

Two other observations about the dearth of women in
"masculine" fields must be added here. First, there is clear
evidence that the absence of women in those fields was not

[14] M. Elizabeth Tidball and Vera Kistiakowsky, "Baccalaureate Origins
of American Scientists and Scholars," *Science*, Vol. 193, No. 4254 (August
20, 1976), pp. 646–652.
[15] Charlotte Williams Conable, *Women at Cornell: The Myth of Equal
Education* (Ithaca, N.Y.: Cornell University Press, 1977).

lost on young girls who might eventually have applied. A survey undertaken in the local junior high school in 1969 showed that of 150 seventh-grade girls responding, 16 reported planning to be veterinarians when they grew up. In interviews later, several of these girls reported that they knew they probably wouldn't make it because "Cornell only lets in two a year." At that time, it was true; two beds were earmarked for first-year women veterinarians. Second, it must be noted that in the fall of 1977 women outnumbered men in the entering class of the New York State College of Veterinary Medicine at Cornell University.

In short, the university identified a bias in the system—and corrected it. That kind of bias, together with the problems in women's heads and those resulting from men's assessment of their potential, has clearly contributed to the segregation of women into womanly jobs at universities.

Are there system problems in industry that contribute to the balkanization of the workforce? Absolutely. The female journalism graduate who six months after graduation finds herself taking dictation from her male classmate whose grades were lower than hers—she knows them well. In magazine publishing, advertising, and many other fields, women were automatically given the typing test as a prerequisite for employment. Still today, many personnel practitioners find it difficult to remember that women should not automatically be considered fit only for that. Nor should men be excluded from consideration for clerical posts.

One of the ironies of the current situation is that men are seemingly finding it easier to move into formerly women's jobs than vice versa. The voice of the long-distance telephone operator is frequently a masculine one today. But there are still comparatively few women climbing telephone poles, despite the encouraging advertising AT&T has undertaken. At the time the advertisement showing an attractive woman atop a pole was made, the company couldn't use a real employee because there were no "women linemen."

Until recently, people taking the Strong Vocational

Interest Test were differentiated by sex, with women receiving a pink form and men a blue one. Testing is an area
fraught with dilemmas for women, as for minorities. A recent study set out to test the hypothesis that the Kuder
Occupational Interest Survey might not be effective with
older women seeking to reenter work because all would
have the same interests. Indeed they did not. The cross-
sex-normed scales turned out to be useful in interpreting
the test results for this group: many proved to have interests
that suggested motivation toward formerly male occupations. These would not have been detected if the results
had been compared only with the results of tests taken by
other women. Seventeen percent of the older women tested
proved to have more in common with men as a group than
with the other women.[16]

Another factor affecting selection is the nature of applicants' recommendations. Personnel consultant Jeannette
Perlman recently told members of a management workshop
that it may no longer be worthwhile to check references.
She gave two reasons: (1) an applicant can have access to
letters written by former employers (the implication being
that a nonconfidential letter would be less trustworthy), and
(2) if managers want to get in touch with former employers
by telephone or letter, they need to ask permission of the
applicant.[17] The fact remains, however, that many industrial organizations still rely on letters of recommendation.

Managers may want to scrutinize letters written for
women, especially those on file in some placement service
for a number of years. Evidence from a study of 1,194 letters
of recommendation written for Ph.D. candidates showed
that bias appeared to be operating there.[18] Women candi-

[16] Carol K. Tittle and Eleanor R. Denker, "Kuder Occupational Interest
Survey: Profiles of Reentry Women," *Journal of Counseling Psychology,*
Vol. 24, No. 4 (July 1977), pp. 293–300.

[17] Jeannette Perlman, quoted in *Women Executives' Bulletin,* No. 517
(September 10, 1977).

[18] Jennie Farley, "Academic Recommendations: Males and Females as
Judges and Judged," *Bulletin of the American Association of University
Professors,* Vol. 64, No. 2 (May 1978), pp. 82–85.

dates had virtually always been identified by marital status before about 1970, in part because of a peculiarity in language. For a male candidate, a professor could write about Mr. Jones (a formal reference) or Jones (more informal) or Robert or Bob (to suggest that he knows the candidate very well). No information about Bob Jones's marital status is conveyed by any of these choices. A female candidate is different in that the formal reference (Mrs. or Miss) does indeed transmit information about the candidate. Calling her Jones was perhaps seen as too brusque and masculine; calling her Roberta or Bobbie might have been misunderstood.

So women's marital status was mentioned routinely (if inadvertently) in letters of recommendation. Similarly, both male and female candidates' appearance was commented on much more often in the past than is the case now. This heartening evidence is shown in Tables 8 and 9.

Table 8. Mention of marital status in letters of recommendation for women, by date written.

Era	Total Letters	Mention of Marital Status	
		Number	Percent
1949–1970	228	174	76
1971–1972	192	112	58
1973	201	63	31
1974–1975	173	31	18
1976–1977	207	25	12

Toward Fair Selection Practices

Managers should recognize that there is clear evidence that women have been discriminated against in the past. This may be changing, to be sure, but the trend is there and well documented. Recognizing the possibility of making biased decisions is a giant step toward correcting them. A

Table 9. Mention of physical appearance in letters of recommendation for women and men, by date written.

Era	Total Letters	Mention of Physical Appearance	
		Number	Percent
1949–1970	246	41	17
1971–1972	213	31	15
1973	208	19	9
1974–1975	181	6	3
1976–1977	213	3	1

second step is to make decisions on a sex-blind basis when possible.

A senior woman professor at a university was appalled to find that women's applications for admission to her graduate program were being considered separately from men's. She instituted the policy of covering up names, so that the committee could base its judgments entirely on merit. Naturally, there were clues that sometimes gave away an applicant's sex—participants in the Girl Scouts seldom turned out to be boys. How did the selection process come out? When applicants were judged on this basis, women earned exactly half of the acceptances. That professor's graduate field is one of the few at her university where women and men are equally represented.

Decision makers can clarify their thoughts by listing selection criteria as specifically as possible and then rating each candidate on each criterion. The person with the highest score is the winner. Personnel managers and others responsible for hiring who take the trouble to make such charts are well advised to keep them. If they are to defend their procedures as fair, concrete evidence of the processes they went through will be much more persuasive than assertions that they chose the best according to their lights. As Rosen and Jerdee have pointed out, the more information decision makers have, the more specific their guidelines, and the more objective their decisions seem to be.[19]

The information they seek should be pertinent. They need not be influenced by letters of recommendation, that, like some of those reviewed for the study cited above, emphasize irrelevancies. It is not necessary to know that a candidate is a "tallish blue-eyed blond" or that she is not "neglecting her family." The information that a woman candidate does not "evoke anxiety and hostility in her male colleagues" or that she is "passionately but not stridently feminist" or that she is "properly aggressive for her sex" tells more about the letter writer than the candidate. We do not need to know that a candidate's devotion to scholarship is "remarkable in a young woman physically so slight and so pretty."

As Hoffman notes, a letter writer can diminish a female candidate's intellectual power by stereotyping her by the way she looks.[20] One recommender did just that when he wrote: "Miss _____ might seem to be too feminine, too pretty, and, in short, too marriageable to be a serious participant in so taxing and demanding a discipline as ours."

What decision makers can do is to specify the work-related criteria they will use and make their judgments solely on those. Everything else, like the footstep behind the screen at the orchestra audition, just gets in the way.

[19] Benson Rosen and Thomas H. Jerdee, "Sex Stereotyping in the Executive Suite," *Harvard Business Review*, Vol. 52, No. 2 (March–April 1974), pp. 45–58.

[20] Nancy Jo Hoffman, "Sexism in Letters of Recommendation: A Case for Consciousness Raising," *Modern Language Association Newsletter*, Vol. 4, No. 4 (September 1972), pp. 5–6.

They don't recognize women as having management potential and they
don't put them on the high-potential
lists, which would enable them to
move up fast.

*—Woman employee of
a major oil company* [1]

5

The Training
Function:
Who Should Be
Learning What?

OF the three personnel functions discussed—recruiting,
selecting, and training—the third may be the least changed
by the new legislation. Recruitment practices are being
modified, even at hidebound universities. There are fewer
job openings in academic life than there were ten years ago,
but information about them has become more accessible.
The number of openings advertised in the *Chronicle of*

---

[1] Cited in Elizabeth M. Fowler, "Careers: Women MBAs Tell of Discrimination," *The New York Times*, June 22, 1977, p. 59.

Higher Education and in at least some other journals grows steadily. Selection practices are, it seems, also being modified and standardized. This may be in part because those participating in decisions know they may well be challenged later and have to defend their procedures after the fact. But training techniques and content have not been overhauled to the same extent.

Three reasons can be advanced for the relative stability of the training function. First, it is a comparatively private activity. There is little public knowledge about or scrutiny of the ways workers learn to do their jobs when they first join a company and less about continuing opportunities that may be open to them. Second, the legislation and guidelines are comparatively vague about how corporations, labor organizations, public agencies, and others can assist members of affected groups to become qualified for advancement.

The spirit of the legislation is clear enough: managers should take reasonable steps to provide whatever training is necessary. As the affirmative action officer in the personnel department of the Bank of America, San Francisco, has pointed out, women employees vary in terms of the kind of training and/or counseling they need. She identifies at least three groups:

1. Those who qualify for and openly aspire to positions in management.
2. Those who qualify for higher positions but due to cultural conditioning do not *think* they can hold officer-level jobs.
3. Those who sincerely do not want to pursue careers.

The woman in the first group is easy to identify and promote when ready; the woman in the third group, honestly happy with her work in her present job, should be recognized as providing valuable service to the organization and not made to feel less valued than her more ambitious co-workers. "The woman in Group 2 presents a challenge. . . . [She] needs to be asked if she wants to take a job with more responsibility. [The supervisor's job] is to recognize this person and give her the confidence and guidance she needs." [2]

Besides confidence, of course, the woman in the second group needs skills, which she can acquire through training. But the kind of training that management should offer to aspiring women is not spelled out in detail in the guidelines or, in fact, in company policy. Therein lies the third reason for the relative stability of the training function despite equal opportunity legislation: lack of solid information about what works.

In truth, little is known about how adults learn, especially about the efficacy of one teaching method over another. As a rule, evaluations of existing programs are based on participants' responses to questionnaires—in other words, on the trainees' reactions rather than on objective measures of the learning that took place. If the evaluations are good, reports on the program are circulated as evidence that there has been a breakthrough. Kay reports, for example, that the marks awarded to one program by participants averaged 9.3, where 9 was "upper good" and 10 "excellent." Naturally, the question arises: Upper good compared to what? It might be that participants would see any program as an improvement over staying at work in the office. One trainee said that the program inspired her to work toward a career goal that had been a "vague dream" before. Another reported that participation made her feel "important to the system" and that she believed her employer cared about its employees. [3] The latter feeling may well have come about just because the woman was chosen for the training and not because of anything that transpired in the program.

[2] Suki Cathey, "Bank of America's Affirmative Action Seminar," in Dorothy Jongeward and Dru Scott (eds.), *Affirmative Action for Women: A Practical Guide* (Reading, Mass.: Addison-Wesley, 1974), pp. 190–191.

[3] Janice Kay, "Career Development for Women: An Affirmative Action First," *Training and Development Journal*, Vol. 30, No. 5 (May 1976), pp. 22–24, p. 22.

To be sure, some programs are easier to evaluate than others. A department investment in a brushup shorthand course for a secretary can be said to have paid off handsomely if the secretary demonstrates improved ability to take dictation back on the job. But management development programs are more difficult to evaluate. Harvard University offers a six-week summer course at its Institute for Educational Management. Participants are presidents of small colleges and top-level administrators at bigger institutions. Their home colleges finance the summer study. People selected for the course are pleased on two counts: their institutions think enough of them to shell out the tuition money and the program itself is highly respected. But the home colleges may not be so respectful when they learn that, according to one analysis, most of the participants leave their institutions within two years of taking the course.

What Kind of Training?

Bolton and Humphreys have reviewed the types of training offered by industrial organizations, from skills courses through time off for study elsewhere to executive development conferences.[4] They conclude that women workers have participated less than men have in every kind of training. Some analysts attribute this to the fact that the woman worker already has a "double day." Because she works for pay and still bears the primary responsibility for housework and child care, she has so much to do that she cannot take on more. Others point to the traditional belief held by managers that women are not good investments (see Chapter 2). Women, it is said, will go through the expensive training program and then, like the participants in

[4] Elizabeth B. Bolton and Luther Wade Humphreys, "A Training Model for Women: An Androgynous Approach," *Personnel Journal,* Vol. 56, No. 5 (May 1977), p. 230.

the Harvard summer institute, leave the organization. For some reason, it seems more difficult for a company to lose its investment when a woman elects to stay home and care for her children than when a man who has been trained leaves the company to join a competitor. As Alice Cook has noted, men who leave an organization to serve in the military have far fewer difficulties when they reenter civilian work than do women who leave the organization to serve society in a different (but at least equally honorable) way: to bear and rear children.

A third explanation given for women's absence from management development conferences on campuses is that, by tradition, companies have sent "bright young men." An older woman, even though thoretically on their level in terms of promotability, may well be overlooked as a potential participant. When such conferences have been male enclaves for years, the introduction of a female may be seen as awkward.

A more reasonable explanation, however, for women's lack of access to training programs is not any male conspiracy to keep them out but the nature of the jobs women hold. Women seldom hold apprenticeships because most work in fields where unions have not penetrated. In the corporate world much thought and planning has been expended on developing executives but little on training clerical workers.[5] Most women are stalled below middle management, where little training is offered.[6]

Alpander has compared the participants in training programs at the University of Maine between 1973 and 1974. During that time, 101 women attended special programs to prepare them for management and 121 men participated in other programs. Their distribution by rank is shown in Table 10. The men's programs were apparently designed

[5] Vera J. Hilliard, "How a Secretarial Training Program Can Increase Company Efficiency," *Personnel Journal*, Vol. 56, No. 8 (August 1977), pp. 410–413.

[6] Margaret Hennig and Anne Jardim, *The Managerial Woman* (Garden City, N.Y.: Doubleday/Anchor, 1977).

for first- and second-line managers, although a few top managers came as well as some nonsupervisory employees and "others"—people who listed themselves as separate from the other categories. Nearly a fifth of the women participants could not fit themselves into any of the categories, perhaps didn't understand them, or perhaps were seeking management training jobs rather than advancement within their companies. It does seem clear that women who have access to management training are more likely to be beginners than men are.

Table 10. Participants in University of Maine training programs, by sex and rank, May 1973 to April 1974.

	Women (N = 101)		Men (N = 121)	
Rank	Number	Percent	Number	Percent
Top management	14	17	19	16
First- and second-line management	16	20	72	60
Nonsupervisory personnel	52	63	10	8
Other	—	—	20	17
	82 [a]	100	121	101 [b]

Source: Adapted from Guvenc G. Alpander and Jean E. Gutmann, "Content and Techniques of Management Development Programs for Women," *Personnel Journal*, Vol. 55, No. 1 (February 1976), Table 1, p. 77.
[a] Only 82 respondents supplied this information from 101 sampled.
[b] Due to rounding.

What kinds of programs should a company be offering to help its employees develop to their full potential? The training department (if one exists) or the personnel generalist is left to make the decision. Sometimes there are considerable restraints on the resources available, and the personnel practitioner is under pressure to make choices that will really pay off. There are three approaches personnel managers can take. First, they can examine the existing job structure and the biographies of the incumbents at each level to determine how people have made their way up in the company before. How do staff members cross over the divide between nonexempt and exempt, if they ever do? How do employees with no relations in top management get up there themselves? Second, personnel managers can ask the staff members what kind of training they want or ask the supervisors what they believe would help others to become supervisors. Third, managers can ask trainers what they are prepared to provide—in other words, they can call on outside experts for guidance. The third method is most often used, it appears. The first, an analysis of current career ladders, is sometimes avoided because of the time and expense involved.

The second approach, asking the employees themselves, does not always achieve the desired result. Some staff members persist in choosing courses of study that managers reject as not sufficiently job-related. Women staff members are, it is said, far too likely to elect group dynamics or self-awareness courses when they should be studying accounting or budgeting. Supervisors have a tendency to overemphasize credentials as requirements for their own jobs, and sometimes their suggestions for training are so out of line that managers turn instead to consultants from outside. They pick and choose among them, sometimes, as we shall see, at their peril.

In the early 1970s traditional training for managers continued to be offered for men. At the same time, a great many programs purporting to train women or to help them were flourishing. A young woman manager in a telephone company looked back ruefully over the year 1976. "They went at training me with a vengeance," she said. "In fact, they sent me on every nut weekend program that came along—I am a very font of experiential learning." Has she gained self-confidence? It does not seem so, because she concluded: "I'm still not sure why they chose to send me on those marathon weekends and other junkets. Do you suppose they think I am too uptight or something?"

A *Money* magazine reporter was equally skeptical of the

two courses she sat in on. "The emphasis on sensitivity training may be misplaced," she wrote, "since women are often accused of being sensitive to a fault." Almost all the other participants rated the courses as valuable. Except one. This person's acerbic comment: " 'Eighty percent of it was a waste of time. . . . It's a con job. I think they prey on people who are naive. If you're that naive, you'll have a hard time getting ahead in the business world.' " [7] A women administrator at Xerox Corp. echoes that sentiment: "We need to disabuse women of two beliefs. The first is that they can keep out of the in-fighting and be above the politics of the business world. Sure they can—but they will just be a pawn in somebody else's game. Winners get in there and fight. And second, we have to help women stop relying on the *Shuddaottawanna* philosophy. You know, that's the view that you can expect people to do things out of the goodness of their hearts; they just *should ought to want to*."

These comments call to mind Veiga's experience with the quality of the advice women give one another. Reflecting on his work with some 400 women in career development seminars, he writes: "One individual's career advice is of little use to others in different circumstances and, more important, it often implies a strategy which acts as a script the individual is not suited to follow." [8]

What Will Training Accomplish?

Personnel managers who sponsor a program for women or minorities—or indeed for men, to educate them about the organization's EEO commitment [9]—should consider first the nature of the program's goals. Is it realistic? The results

[7] "C.D.," "A Firsthand Report from the Seminar Circuit," *Money*, August 1976, p. 32.

[8] John F. Veiga, "Female Career Myopia," *Human Resource Management*, Vol. 15, No. 4 (Winter 1976), pp. 24–27, p. 24.

[9] Gloria Gery, "Equal Opportunity Planning and Managing the Process of Change," *Personnel Journal*, Vol. 56, No. 4 (April 1977), pp. 184–203.

of a social psychologists' experiment suggest the folly of imagining that any campaign of propaganda alone will change behavior. The experiment was undertaken by the Sherifs at a boys' summer camp known as Robbers' Cave. The first day at camp, the incoming boys tended to pair off. The experimenters encouraged the boys to make friends but then divided the campers into two groups, carefully separating each pair of friends. Next the psychologists set about to create bad feelings between the two teams. With surprisingly few interventions (for example, disarranging one team's gear and leading the members to think the other team did it), a classic case of intergroup conflict developed. The boys called one another names; each team developed an ugly stereotype about the other; members of the two teams refused to sit together or eat together, or indeed to be integrated in any way.

The experimenters found it more difficult than they had imagined to end the conflict they had set in motion. Attempts at integration failed. They tried mediation. No success. An educational campaign seemingly had no effect at all, even when the experimenters revealed that the conflict had all been planned. How did the boys react to the news that in fact the other team was composed of people they had chosen as friends the first day? By saying that they hadn't realized at the time how *rotten* those other guys were. The experimenters attempted to impose a threat from outside, in the hopes that the two teams would close ranks, as adults do in war. Indeed, when the campers at Robbers' Cave were in competition in some sport with campers from elsewhere, antagonisms were set aside. But once the visiting campers left, the hostilities resumed. Only when the experimenters devised a task that required the two teams to work together toward a common goal did intergroup relations improve. Then the integration effort began to work and the educational campaign, to "take."

One implication of the Robbers' Cave experiments is that it is not sufficient to tell men that the law requires that equal opportunity be made available to women. It won't take. Nor will it help to automatically channel all women into assertiveness training, commanding them to be "assertive, not aggressive." Putnam has noted that we give confusing and contradictory advice to women. There is not only the classic situation that male managers identify aggressiveness as an important trait for managers on the one hand and, on the other, count it as unattractive in women—even as they assure all within hearing that they are "for women." More important, Putnam feels, much of the counsel given to aspiring women is based on acceptance of an antiquated "trait theory" of leadership—that if women will just act this way or that way, they will be as good as leaders as men are. The fact is, she notes, that good leaders respond to situations inventively. That is the kind of behavior we should encourage, not some artificial set of male-defined traits like dominance and aggressiveness.[10]

It is equally naive to believe that any training program will move a substantial number of women from the bottom rungs of the career ladder. Career education, advocated so earnestly by many as the panacea for women's woes,[11] seems to be of considerably less value for schoolgirls than for schoolboys.[12] Even sending a manager back to earn an MBA may be of limited value if the goal is to sensitize the manager to EEO problems. By one professor's account, male faculty members in business schools still don't take women's problems seriously enough to include materials in the regular curriculum. The male students react with hostility to any information that is presented: despite this, the female students feel there is no real problem for women

[10] Linda Putnam and J. Stephen Heinen, "Women in Management: The Fallacy of the Trait Approach," *Michigan State University Business Topics*, Vol. 24, No. 3 (Summer 1976), pp. 47–53.

[11] Anita M. Mitchell, "Facilitating Full Employment of Women Through Career Education," in *American Women Workers in a Full Employment Economy*, report to the Joint Economic Committee, U.S. Congress, September 15, 1977, pp. 195–202.

[12] Frank L. Mott and Sylvia F. Moore, "The Determinants and Consequences of Occupational Information for Young Women," preliminary report, Center for Human Resource Research, College of Administrative Science, The Ohio State University, April 1976.

who are *good* in these liberated times. Furthermore, the
women students don't want to be identified with solely
"women's concerns," in part because they fear being
stereotyped as "women's libbers." And the women faculty?
At graduate business schools they are few and far between.[13]

There is disagreement as to whether the single-sex class
or the coeducational one will be more effective. Halas argues for all women's groups; [14] most others favor the integrated setting.[15] There is agreement, however, that the lone
woman in an all-male group is in trouble. Wolman and
Frank show evidence that a woman sees herself—and is
seen by her co-trainees—as less competent when she is
isolated.[16] Kanter provides a list of the troubles encountered by the new group member who is seen as deviant—
that evidence alone is enough to persuade us that it is a
miracle that Jackie Robinson survived.[17]

At entry, a woman often does find herself alone, no matter what the company's motive for hiring her. A decade of
experience in Sweden, as reported by Alice Cook, has convinced managers there that women entering traditionally
male trades feel very alone indeed. Counseling and
support—especially in the first three months—are vital in
helping women hang on until they get used to the unfamiliar setting. Basing her comments on the work of Rita Liljes-
trøm, Cook notes that, as a rule, it is older women, not
young girls, who try to enter "men's jobs." Young women
just in the process of establishing their sexual identity may

[13] Ronald J. Burke and Tamara Weir, "Readying the Sexes for Women in
Management," *Business Horizons,* Vol. 20, No. 3 (June 1977), pp. 30–35.
[14] Celia Halas, "All-Women's Groups—A View from Inside," *Personnel
and Guidance Journal,* Vol. 52, No. 2 (October 1973), pp. 91–95.
[15] Alma S. Baron, "Special Training Course for Women: Desirable or
Not?" *Training and Development Journal,* Vol. 30, No. 12 (December
1976), pp. 30–33. See also Bolton and Humphreys, *passim.*
[16] Carol Wolman and Hal Frank, "The Sole Woman in a Professional
Peer Group," Working Paper 138, Department of Management, The Whar-
ton School, University of Pennsylvania, September 1972.
[17] Rosabeth Moss Kanter, *Men and Women of the Corporation* (New
York: Basic Books, 1977).

find it too threatening to take on so-called men's work at that time in their lives. We can speculate that the older woman, perhaps a divorcée with children to support, is both more secure in her identity as a woman and more needy; she cannot afford the luxury of worrying about "losing her femininity" when she needs the extra pay.

Another method of combatting the isolation women feel is to include women among the trainers. A junior staff member was invited, at company expense, to attend a summer seminar for executives on a university campus. She felt honored to be invited until she checked over the brochure, the list of faculty, and the group picture from the year before. With a sinking heart, she realized that she'd be the only woman "on retreat" with 59 men for six weeks. She had first thought, "What a great chance for somebody!" but on reflection she concluded, "It would have to be somebody else, not me." Had she gone, she would have found, perhaps, that the materials were entirely male-oriented. The "in basket" exercises included not one woman manager; indeed, the case studies said nothing about the woman worker—recruiting her, selecting her, training her, promoting her.

It is clear that the materials used in traditional training courses will have to be modified.[18] Such revised material will be instructive for both sexes. It appears too that both sexes profit from an entry program that is larger than two or three people [19] and that is directed toward preparing managers to cope with hazing practices.[20] The evidence to date suggests that training programs for women and men should be based on the model that has proved to work for male

[18] Guvenc G. Alpander and Jean E. Gutmann, "Content and Techniques of Management Development Programs for Women," *Personnel Journal*, Vol. 55, No. 1 (February 1976), pp. 76–79.

[19] William M. Evan. "Peer-Group Interaction and Organizational Socialization: A Study of Employee Turnover," *American Sociological Review*, Vol. 28, No. 3 (June 1963), pp. 436–440.

[20] Earl R. Gomersall and M. Scott Meyers, "Breakthrough in On-the-Job-Training," *Harvard Business Review*, Vol. 44, No. 4 (July–August 1966), pp. 62–72.

managers, insofar as evaluation can be trusted. Special programs for teaching women to become more assertive are unnecessary because only some women (and men) have that problem. Similarly, special programs designed to make women something many already are—sensitive to the needs of others—may well be of limited value, not to say a prime ripoff.

Finally, if upper middle management is a male domain, perhaps what women need is an integrated version of the in-house executive trainee programs favored by many companies. Women are often specialists, experts in their own fields in the company, but quite ignorant of the way their work fits into the big picture. If they can join the male trainees in moving from department to department, they too may get a valuable overview of the company and its aims.

A Larger View of Training and Development

If the ultimate aim of training is to assist employees in making the best possible contribution to the organization, it seems clear that an array of offerings is desirable. Not all problems in production or morale can be solved by sending employees to school. But some can. Hilliard paints a vivid picture of the harassed male manager, sinking under a wave of disorganized paper, frantically trying to keep up with his sliding piles of telephone messages, memos, and reports to complete. Meantime, his secretary at her desk outside is on the phone with her friend down the hall, complaining that others got raises and she didn't. In such a situation, Hilliard holds, the institution of a training program—planned with input from clerical workers, approved by management, and limited to specific objectives—can improve secretaries' efficiency.[21]

Such a program will, in fact, be in line with development programs designed for other employees (mainly

---

[21] Hilliard, p. 413.

males) at other levels in the workforce. Programs for workers of both sexes may be innovative not only in the choice of
groups served but in the time of life they are offered. Gulf
Oil has planned a program to provide those holding the
bachelor of arts in chemistry with some of the skills and
applied expertise of chemical engineers. Older women as
well as new graduates are among those seen as suitable
participants.

The New York State Regents have initiated a business
training program for graduate students in the humanities
and so-called soft social sciences. New Ph.D.s are being
offered a summer crash course in business at the New York
University graduate School of Business. Participants meet
with representatives of life insurance companies, banks,
and other corporate institutions. The aim is to place these
women and men in mainstream jobs in business and
industry—not in special "poet in residence" jobs created
for them. It is felt that the new doctorates can make a valuable contribution to the business world. The program may
also support the thesis that their graduate education can be
utilized in fields other than traditional research and college
teaching, where jobs become less available each academic
year.

The *Women Executives' Bulletin* outlines a program to
teach prospective managers bargaining techniques to assist
them in dealing with supervisors and co-workers.[22] As one
woman manager said, "I had to beat down my reluctance to
ask for a fur coat when what I really wanted was a pea jacket
when I first came on this job. I wish somebody had told me
in advance that this is the way it works around here."

Wesleyan University and Wellesley College are among a
number of institutions experimenting with courses and
clinics and support programs in mathematics for people
who think they hate mathematics. Sociologist Lucy Sells at
the University of California at Berkeley was among the first

[22] "Winning Through Compromise," *Woman Executive's Bulletin*, No.
520 (October 25, 1977), pp. 3–6.

to discover that women and men entering college differed greatly in their academic preparation in math. The men were much more likely to offer advanced high school math credits than the women were. As a result, Sells reports, the majority of majors open to entering freshmen were in fact essentially closed to women, unless they undertook remedial work. Few chose to. This meant, in turn, that a whole range of jobs were forever closed to them. Sheila Tobias, associate provost at Wesleyan, has noted that when many young women respond to questions about their aspirations with the statement "I want to work with people," what they may really be saying is "I am no good at math." Registration at the Math Anxiety Clinics has shown that some men suffer from this malady as well, but it appears to be more prevalent among women.

One difference between freshman women engineers and their male counterparts is not that either group fears mathematics or feels anxious about their abilities in that realm but that women have had less "hands on" experience with machinery than men have. To remedy this, the College of Engineering at Cornell offered a remedial laboratory skills course for women to assist them in catching up to their male classmates. The program was deemed very successful, but it ran into two classic problems. First, some felt it might well be in violation of university policy against segregating classes by sex. That defect was remedied by opening it to men. Then the second problem arose: the course became overcrowded and too big to accomplish its purpose. Now the course is divided into a women's section and a men's.

Best and Stern maintain that training—both formal and informal education—can enrich the lives of women and men of all ages. They note that the conventional path people follow (attending school in youth and early adulthood, working in the middle years, and retiring in old age) puts needless restrictions on the full development of human potential. In an enlightened society, they hold, the activities of learning, working, and enjoying leisure would be alternated throughout the life cycle. Such a reorganization of society would be liberating for both sexes; it would also increase the range of choices for the individual.[23] Safilios-Rothschild has summed up the current situation as the "all-or-nothing model of employment and achievement." People who want time off for retraining or those contemplating midcareer change are penalized, as are those who choose to combine study and work in their middle years.[24]

Setting Up a Training Program

The research cited in this chapter suggests certain characteristics that effective programs appear to share: They are planned for a specific group, have limited goals, have both women and men as teachers, and are open to both sexes yet slanted exclusively toward neither. Both the traditional model of male teachers teaching male trainees with male-oriented materials and the substitute model of all-women's groups, concentrating solely on developing sensitivity or assertiveness, have proven to be inadequate.

Let us consider a proposal for a program that would, it is hoped, avoid both of these pitfalls. A company seeking to serve its employees at all levels might well offer a program for people who want to quit smoking. This would be in line with various exercise, diet, and nutrition programs offered from time to time.

Why should the company find it in its self-interest to promote such a program? The deleterious effect of nicotine addiction on work behavior has been little studied,[25] but

[23] Fred Best and Harry Stern, "Education, Work, and Leisure: Must They Come in That Order?" *Monthly Labor Review*, Vol. 100, No. 7 (July 1977), pp. 3–10.

[24] Constantina Safilios-Rothschild, "Women and Work: Policy Implications and Prospects for the Future," in Ann H. Stromberg and Shirley Harkess (eds.), *Women Working: Theories and Facts in Perspective* (Palo Alto, Cal.: Mayfield, 1977), pp. 419–433.

[25] Harrison M. Trice and Paul M. Roman, *Spirits and Demons at Work: Alcohol and Other Drugs on the Job* (Ithaca, N.Y.: New York State School of Industrial and Labor Relations, Cornell University, 1972), p. 140.

there is solid evidence that smokers lose more days at work and have more health problems of all kinds than do nonsmokers.[26] The program would be designed to appeal to both women and men. Evidence to date suggests strongly that women have more difficulty quitting and a higher relapse rate than men do. At the same time, women appear to be more vulnerable than men to certain health risks associated with smoking. Simply outlining the risks—that is, education alone (as in the Robbers' Cave experiments)—does not bring about the desired results. Indeed, among both smokers and nonsmokers, women are already more likely than men to agree with the statement that smoking is dangerous to health.[27]

The need appears clear. How shall the program be designed? A first step is to find (or, if necessary, develop) materials that will be as relevant for women as for men. Second, it is important to find teachers of both sexes. Third, it seems vital to establish a balance between the sexes and races to maximize the benefits for all participants and make them feel at ease.

The aim of such a training program is not necessarily to increase employees' sensitivity to problems of women and minorities, to give them the skills they need to climb from one job to another, or to acquaint them with the workings of departments other than their own. Instead, its goal is modest: to help people who want to quit smoking to either do so or cut down drastically. It won't transform their lives but it might lengthen them. Employers might well consider the long-range gains of beginning where missionaries do: with health. In any case, the training dollar would be more soundly invested in a nonsmoking workforce than in a workforce with heavy smokers.

[26] Daniel Horn, "The Health Consequences of Smoking," in Edgar F. Borgatta and Robert Evans (eds.), *Smoking, Health, and Behavior* (Chicago: Aldine, 1968), pp. 52–80. See also "Smoking and Health: Report of the Advisory Committee to the Surgeon General of the Public Health Service" (Washington, D.C.: U.S. Department of Health, Education, and Welfare, 1964).

[27] Edward M. Brecher et al., *Licit and Illicit Drugs* (Boston: Little, Brown, 1972), p. 234.

Such a program for employees at all levels may have a number of beneficial side effects. Employees may feel greater sympathy for one another's problems; communication channels among departments may become unclogged. Virtually every participant will gain some empathy for the work situation of fellow trainees. And antagonism between the sexes may diminish when men and women work together to solve a common problem.

The training function has not changed as drastically in response to EEO legislation as selection and recruitment have. But it is clearly to the advantage of management that training programs be modified. When the workforce cannot be enlarged, training is of increased importance.[28] Poor training programs for women waste the corporate dollar just as surely as poor programs for men. Similarly, there is the recurring problem of encouraging appropriate groups to take them. Here, as in recruiting efforts, it is fatally easy to make employees feel that the programs are the same as ever and thus discourage women and minorities from even applying. Perhaps there is a clear lesson in the trend toward posting job openings at all levels, which permits individual employees to study the requirements and then decide whether to apply for a position. Similarly, open publicity about training opportunities would permit members of affected groups to identify their needs and aspirations, instead of waiting until some supervisor passes them the word in confidence or taps them for training. The decision about whether to accept an individual will still be (and should be) made by management, but the negotiations can surely be opened by the worker.

If training needs are assessed systematically, as De-Cotiis and Morano suggest,[29] the decision about who to train can be made without regard to sex of trainee. What skills does it take to be a mail carrier? Asking the question

---

[28] Francine S. Hall, "Gaining EEO Compliance with a Stable Workforce," *Personnel Journal*, Vol. 56, No. 9 (September 1977), pp. 454–457.

[29] Thomas A. DeCotiis and Richard A Morano, "Applying Job Analysis to Training," *Training and Development Journal*, Vol. 31. No. 7 (July 1977), pp. 20–24.

that way led Armco Steel Corp. to open up that job at its Middletown plant to women, something that had never been permitted before. "The job was considered for men because the carriers must go into every part of the mill." [30] Women can indeed be taught to do that too.

There is renewed interest in training at all levels, as evidenced by a facility recently opened by the New England Telephone & Telegraph Co.[31] The handsome new building is in a campuslike setting; it is designed for middle managers in operations as opposed to technical specialists. It is one of the first in the country in that respect. If only that beautiful building included a child care center, it would truly represent a breakthrough in training for women as well as for men.

[30] Donna Witte, "Women at Armco in 'Man's World' Winning Respect," *Middletown (Ohio) Journal,* July 17, 1977.
[31] Vilma Barr, "Management Training in Its Own Campus Setting," *Training and Development Journal,* Vol. 31, No. 7 (July 1977), pp. 47–48.

As white women move out of their houses, who'll do their housework and take care of their children? As the white women move up at work, who'll get the boring, low-paid jobs they leave behind? You don't know who. But I do. So I say to you, for every "white lady" you liberate, don't exploit one of my black sisters.

—*Comment at a women's conference on going back to work*

6

The Minority Woman: Doubly Protected

IN 1965 President Lyndon B. Johnson issued Executive Order 11246, requiring that firms doing business with the government act differently to prevent discrimination on the basis of race, color, religion, or national origin. To be sure, the phrase "minority group" as used in the executive order included American Indians, Japanese, Chinese, Filipinos, Koreans, and all other American citizens except majority whites. But most Americans thought Johnson was seeking to protect the rights of 7 percent of the population: black men. And he probably was. Three years later, the order was amended to include women. This caused a linguistic problem at first. One couldn't say "blacks, women, and other minorities," because women outnumber men in the population. For clarity, the protected groups were identified as "minorities and women." A great many people believed that, as the original executive order was really supposed to protect black men, so the amendment was meant to expand the coverage to include women: *white* women, that is.

One group of citizens was forgotten—black women—until it occurred to somebody that the categories overlapped. There are, in fact, people who are both women and members of minority groups, and they are covered twice. This was the subject of jokes in the early 1970s; but citizens whose lives were shaped by two factors over which they had no control—their race and their sex—seldom found the jokes amusing. And for good reason.

The Black Woman's Situation

Black women as a group have always suffered from higher unemployment than black men; they earn less than either white women or black men, as shown in Tables 11 and 12. One reason for the high unemployment rate and the low median wage of black Americans of both sexes is their

Table 11. Median earnings of year-round full-time workers, by sex and race, 1972.

White men	$10,593
Black men	7,301
White women	5,998
Black women	5,147

Source: *Minority Women and Higher Education*, No. 1 (Washington, D.C.: Association of American Colleges, n.d.), p. 4.

Table 12. Unemployment rates, by sex and race, 1973.

White men	4.3
White women	5.3
Black men	7.9
Black women	11.1

Source: Ibid.

relative lack of education. This limitation has crippled women more than men. There are many beliefs about black women's educational status that are commonly accepted but do not deserve to be. The Project on the Status and Education of Women has identified some of the misconceptions as follows: [1]

The Myth	*The Reality*
1. "Black women have always been more educated than black men."	1. It was not until 1940 that black women caught up to their brothers in terms of schooling. By the middle 1960s, 6 percent of black women aged 34 or younger had completed college, as opposed to 5 percent of black men.
2. "Black women are increasing their average level of education more rapidly than black men."	2. The median education level of black women is increasing more slowly than that of their brothers. Between 1966 and 1972, the median level for black women rose a year; for black men, a year and a half. Both lag behind whites, with the white male at 12.4 years, the white female at 12.3, the black male at 10.9, and the black female at 11.1.
3. "Black males are much more likely to be high school dropouts than black females."	3. As of 1973, young black men and women were dropping out of school at approximately the same rate.

[1] *Minority Women and Higher Education*, No. 1 (Washington, D.C.: Association of American Colleges, n.d.), pp. 1–3.

The Myth	*The Reality*
4. "Black women outnumber black men on the campuses."	4. In 1973, 19 percent of black men between the ages of 18 and 24 were students, versus 14 percent of black women.
5. "Black women are not 'serious' about college: they don't stay long enough to obtain degrees."	5. Black college women are more likely to complete their bachelor's degrees in four years than their brothers.
6. "Black women aren't ambitious. They don't really want a college education."	6. In 1971, black women appeared to be more ambitious than the other freshmen surveyed by the American Council on Education: 62 percent of the black female freshmen rated themselves as above average in "drive to achieve," compared with 59 percent of the black males. (Of the nonblacks, 53 percent of the women and 51 percent of the men gave themselves that rating.)
7. "A high percentage of blacks who hold doctorates are women."	7. As of 1969, 95 percent of the doctorates earned by blacks were awarded to men. Of all doctorates awarded by U.S. institutions, about 88 percent went to men.
8. "Once black men achieve full equality, black women won't 'need' as much education."	8. Well over a third of black families are headed by women—and the proportion is rising.

It is clear that black women are disadvantaged in terms of education. It once was the case that black parents favored educating a daughter over a son, perhaps knowing that she could find work as a teacher in a black institution in an era when men who graduated from Howard University were still working as sleeping-car porters. Now, it appears, black sons are favored, as white sons have always been. White families have always deemed it essential that boys get schooling, since they will have to work. Girls, it has been presumed, would find husbands to take care of them. Black families have seldom had the illusion that their children of either sex would be supported by anybody other than themselves.

For every age group except teenagers, the labor force participation of black women has always been higher than that of white women. Among teenage black women, the unemployment rate is currently approaching 50 percent, the highest rate suffered by any group. Overall, however, black women have always been more likely to work than white women. In 1948, 46 percent of all black females aged 16 or more were working; by 1974 this percentage had risen to 48 percent. Of white women, in contrast, 31 percent were working in 1948; that proportion rose to 45 percent by 1974.[2] It is clear, then, that black women are less educated than their white sisters, yet more likely to be working or looking for work.

Black women's situation differs from that of majority women in other ways: life expectancy, marital status, and likelihood of living in poverty. Black women live longer than their brothers, just as white women outlive white men, as a group. But the gap is wider for blacks than for whites: the minority man has the shortest life, statistically speaking, of any American. White males have an average life expectancy of 68.9 years; white females, 76.6 years; minority males, 62.9 years; and minority females, 71.2 years.[3]

[2] *1975 Handbook on Women Workers* (Washington, D.C.: U.S. Department of Labor, 1975), p. 41.
[3] *Statistical Abstract of the United States* (Washington, D.C.: U.S. Department of Commerce, 1976), p. 61.

In part because of this demographic reality, black women are less likely to be married and living with their husbands than are white women. In 1973, 61 percent of black women were married and living with husbands, compared with 78 percent of white women. Blacks and other minority women who are married and living with their husbands are more likely to be working than are their single, divorced, or widowed sisters. In contrast, white married women are less likely to work than are *their* unmarried sisters.[4] Finally, although the majority of women receiving public assistance are white, a greater proportion of black women as a group are in poverty than of white women as a group.

The black woman typically holds a different kind of job from her white sister, as shown in Table 13. The occupational distribution for white women has changed little from 1963. There has been a substantial change, however, for black women. In 1968 more than 33 percent were in private household work, while only 10 percent were in clerical work. Thus differences in the occupational distribution of women by race are narrowing. A substantial proportion of

Table 13. Women's labor force participation, by occupational group and race, 1973.

Occupational Group	White Women	Minority Women
Clerical	36%	25%
Service work	17	25
Professional and technical	14	13
Operatives	13	16
Private household workers	4	14
All other occupations	16	7
	100%	100%

Source: Adapted from *1975 Handbook on Women Workers* (Washington, D.C.: U.S. Department of Labor, 1975), Chart J, p. 103.

[4] *Minority Women Workers: A Statistical Overview* (Washington, D.C.: U.S. Department of Labor, 1977 rev.).

black women moved from domestic service to clerical work, making their pattern much more similar to that of white women than it had been before.

We have seen, then, that black women as a group have high unemployment, a high labor force participation rate, a low median wage, a comparatively low level of education, a life expectancy higher than men's but lower than white women's, and a pattern of participating in clerical, service, and unskilled factory jobs.

Attitudes toward Work

There is solid evidence that black women are well aware of the necessity to work. In 1967 Fichter found that black college women were more likely to anticipate using their education at work than were white women. He noted, in fact, that black college men also expected women to work and that there was more agreement on that issue between the sexes among blacks than among whites.[5] As to level of expectation, most researchers have found that black women have higher occupational goals than black men do, although some evidence goes the other way.[6]

Between 1972 and 1976 some 1,384 undergraduates in both black and white institutions of higher education were surveyed. Women in each setting were more likely to mention aspiring to professional-level work than men were. Their responses differed from men's in another way: they were much more likely to mention marriage as part of their future plans. One question dealt with the expected major source of life satisfaction. The question was worded as follows:

[5] Father Joseph H. Fichter, "Marriage and Motherhood of Black Women Graduates," in Nona Glazer-Malbin and Helen Youngelson Waehrer (eds.), *Woman in a Man-Man World: A Socioeconomic Handbook* (Chicago: Rand McNally, 1972), pp. 203–207.

[6] See, for example, Herbert S. Parnes et al., *Years for Decision* (Washington, D.C.: U.S. Department of Labor, 1971). For a contrasting view, see Patricia Gurin and Carolyn Gaylord, "Educational and Occupational Goals of Men and Women at Black Colleges," *Monthly Labor Review*, Vol. 99, No. 6 (June 1976), pp. 10–16.

What three things or activities in your life do you expect
to give you the most satisfaction? Please rank the three in
order of importance (1 being the most important):

_____ Participation as a citizen in the affairs of your com-
munity
_____ Religious beliefs or activities
_____ Career or occupation
_____ Leisure-time recreational activities
_____ Family relationships
_____ Participation in activities directed toward national
or international betterment
_____ Other

The patterns of response by sex and race are shown in
Table 14. The data suggest that college setting (coeducational versus single-sex institution) seems to make as much
or more difference than either sex or race. It appears, then,
that for women mention of family as a major source of life
satisfaction is not linked directly with the low salary expectation women express.

To what extent do women and men differ in salary expectation? Respondents were asked the question this way:
"Please estimate roughly what you will be earning ten
years after your college graduation. Approximately $_____
per year." Responses are shown in Table 15.

It can be seen that high willingness to respond is linked
with high salary expectation. It is also clear that men anticipate higher earnings than women do and that black students expect more than white students do. For every dollar
a white college man anticipates, his female classmate anticipates 72¢; for every dollar a black college man anticipates, his female classmate expects 77¢. At present, black
women earn 72 percent of black men's earnings—quite
close to the pay gap they, as a group, predict for the future.
White women, in contrast, now earn 43 percent of white
men's salaries and predict that they will earn 72 percent of
what men earn within ten years. Black women can be said
to be (depending on how one views the prospects for
change) either more realistic or less optimistic than white

Table 14. Family relationships versus career as expected major source of life satisfaction.

Group	Year Surveyed	Setting	Family First	Career First
White women	1972	Coed university	51%	21%
Black women	1976	Coed university	46	29
White men	1972	Coed university	43	26
White women	1974	Women's college	42	29
Black women	1976	Women's college	34	36
Black men	1976	Coed university	33	31

Source: Jennie Farley, June H. Brewer, and Susan W. Fine, "Black Women's Career Aspirations," *Journal of Employment Counseling*, Vol. 14, No. 3, Table 2, p. 118.

Table 15. Students' estimated future income.

Group	Year Surveyed	Setting	Number	Response [a]	Average Income Expected [b]
White women	1974	Women's college	173	58%	$20,247
White women	1972	Coed university	241	65	20,466
Black women	1976	Women's college	119	73	23,151
Black women	1976	Coed university	128	76	23,219
White men	1972	Coed university	594	82	28,550
Black men	1976	Coed university	129	84	29,980

Source: Farley, Brewer, and Fine, p. 117.
[a] Percentage of those who answered this question.
[b] Figures from 1972 and 1974 corrected at rate of 6 percent per year to 1976 dollars.

women. Others may think of the black woman college graduate as having a special edge in the job market. She does not.

Black Liberation and Women's Liberation

The relationship between black liberation and women's liberation has often been strained, sometimes causing a conflict of loyalties for black women. The history of these two social movements has been entwined. American women were among the first to call for the abolition of slavery; indeed, it was the realization that they couldn't be effective in that struggle because they were women that prompted some of them to think for the first time about discrimination based on sex. As early as 1830 white women were forming organizations to bring about the abolition of slavery. Ten years later abolitionists Lucretia Mott and Elizabeth Cady Stanton attended the World Antislavery Convention in London. The convention ruled that those two delegates could not be seated because they were women. They were relegated to a special section. One man from the American delegation joined them, leaving his seat (and yielding up his privilege as a delegate) on principle. It was a famous journalist: William Lloyd Garrison. He was joined by a black American man: Charles Remond. There were male allies of the women's cause even then.[7]

Eight years later, in 1848, in Seneca Falls, New York, Mott and Stanton sponsored the first conference ever held on equal rights for women. From that time until 1920, reformers campaigned tirelessly to get the vote. The suffragists allied themselves with the abolitionists for the first two decades, seeing the two causes as linked. But a split developed in 1867 when those seeking to get the vote for blacks recognized that the even less popular issue of

---

[7] Eleanor Flexner, *Century of Struggle: The Woman's Rights Movement in the United States* (New York: Atheneum, 1974), pp. 42, 71, 347n.

women's rights was holding them back. The feminists were outraged when even their ally Frederick Douglass deserted them, declaring, "This is the Negro's hour." Elizabeth Cady Stanton countered by saying, "No, no, this is the hour to press women's claims. . . . Enfranchise [only the black man] and we are left outside with lunatics, idiots, and criminals for another twenty years." [8]

She was correct in her prophecy that giving black men the vote would not insure emancipation for women. The Fifteenth Amendment, granting a citizen the right to vote regardless of his race, was proposed in 1869 and proclaimed in 1870. But Stanton was incorrect in the amount of time women's suffrage would take: it was a full 50 years before the passage of the Nineteenth Amendment, granting all American women the right to vote. There had been a powerful voice calling for consideration of the rights of black women: the itinerant preacher and ex-slave Sojourner Truth. She is remembered for her ringing call in 1851 for the inclusion of black women in the feminist movement (". . . and ain't I a woman?"). In 1867 she was to plead with equal eloquence for the inclusion of women in the campaign for black rights, saying: "I am glad to see men getting their rights but I want women to get theirs. . . . Man is so selfish that he has got women's rights and his own too, and yet he won't give women theirs." [9]

After each of the two groups had earned suffrage, the movements languished. It was not until the 1960s that black civil rights again became a national issue: the late 1960s and early 1970s saw the rise of the "new feminists." The two movements have much in common, but they differ in terms of their size, their history, the status of their members, and the support they receive from those whose claims they press. As has been noted, blacks make up 14 percent of the total population and black and white women, 52 per-

---

[8] William O'Neill, *Everyone Was Brave: The Rise and Fall of Feminism in America* (Chicago: Quadrangle Books, 1969), p. 17.

[9] Gerda Lerner, *The Female Experience: An American Documentary* (Indianapolis: Bobbs-Merrill, 1977), pp. 487–489.

cent. Women are many; blacks, few. The history of the two groups has been dissimilar in that blacks have suffered more physical violence at the hands of whites. And the status of the members of the two groups has been different in that black people have had little education as a group.

Women have had more access to schooling historically than blacks. As has been demonstrated, however, women's education has been limited in many respects, some of which were unnoticed until recently. Women are close to men; men in power have mothers, sisters, daughters, wives. When women as a group set out to change their status, there were some influential public figures—women editors, women professors, women writers, and others—who were at least potential allies. Black men and women had fewer highly placed advocates. There were a few—like Franklin Frazier, Martin Luther King, Frederick Douglass, and the graduates of the distinguished Dunbar High School in Washington, D.C.—who had brilliant careers in public service.[10] But the majority of black people had little access to education.

Cross has delineated a four-step process by which a black American moves from a realization of the nature of his situation to a decision to take action on behalf of his people: pre-encounter, encounter, immersion, and internalization.[11] Jo-Ann Evans Gardner, founder of KNOW, Inc., a women's publishing house, uses a somewhat different model to delineate the process by which a woman becomes a feminist. As an example, she cites a woman Ph.D. in psychology who finds herself relegated to marginal jobs in academic life. At first, Gardner contends, the woman tends to think that judgments about her ability must be correct; otherwise, she would have access to the good jobs men have. Only after she comes together with other women who

[10] Jervis Anderson, "Our Far-Flung Correspondents: A Very Special Monument: Dunbar High School," *The New Yorker*, Vol. 54, No. 5 (March 20, 1978), pp. 93–121.

[11] William E. Cross, Jr., "The Negro-to-Black Conversion Experience," in Joyce Ladner (ed.), *The Death of White Sociology*, pp. 267–286.

recount the same experiences does she begin to think of the problem as social rather than personal. "All those women can't be less talented than all those men," she reasons. And she is moved to action. As her feminist consciousness develops, she becomes sensitive to the problems of minorities as well.

This analysis has been criticized by feminists who hold that women are typically sensitized to the oppression of minorities *before* they come to realize that women as a group are in trouble. Whatever the sequence, it appears that women of all races and minority men are alike in that the conversion experience changes them profoundly.

An example of changing group image can be seen in the adoption of group names. Early in our history, black people were known informally as "niggers" and formally as "Negroes," later as "colored people" (as in the NAACP): then, in a wave of black nationalism, as "Afro-Americans"; and most recently as "blacks." Similarly, the first organizations for women in this country used the word "ladies" (as in ladies' auxiliaries); next came "women"; then a brief reliance on the clinical-sounding "female" (as in the wording of the legislation about minorities and females); and most recently a reversion to "women" (as in the National Organization for Women).

As black males resent being called boys, so many women (both young and old) take umbrage at being called girls, gals, chicks. One indicator that the women's rights movement is behind civil rights in terms of acceptance: jokes are still made publicly about women that would be seen as unacceptable if they were about blacks. The name of the movement itself is often shortened to "women's lib," "gals' lib," "femlib"—diminutives that make some feminists gnash their teeth. They remark that nobody would speak of "blackies' lib," and it is devoutly to be hoped that they are correct.

The black woman often finds herself a victim of conflicting loyalties. In the late 1960s many black women defined themselves as black first and women second. At a 1969 con-

ference one black undergraduate made her position clear
when she said she didn't think blacks should be joining any
"women's liberation" effort with whites. "Personally, I
think it is not my problem that your man is oppressing
you." [12] Her first priority, she said, was to put the black man
back at the head of the family.

Black women's groups are still divided over whether to
ally themselves with feminist causes. In July 1976, when 39
major women's magazines in the United States published
articles to stimulate debate on the equal rights amendment,
the black women's magazine *Essence* was among those giving ERA the least coverage. Nevertheless, some were
coming to agree with Representative Shirley Chisholm,
the first black woman to be elected to Congress, who wrote
in 1970:

> Being black is much less of a drawback than being female
> because [eliminating sex prejudice] will be a longer
> struggle. Part of the problem is that women in America
> are much more brainwashed and content with their roles
> as second-class citizens than blacks ever were. . . . The
> happy homemaker and the contented darkey are both
> stereotypes produced by prejudice. [13]

Chisholm was echoing a sentiment expressed some 100
years earlier by Elizabeth Cady Stanton. Both blacks and
women sigh and groan in their chains, Stanton wrote, but
the woman "looks to heaven [for deliverance] whilst the
more philosophical slave sets out for Canada." [14]

There were still dissenting voices. Dorothy Bolden,
founder of the Black Women's Caucus in Atlanta and a
model project called National Domestic Workers, Inc.,
holds that

[12] Alexis De Veaux, as quoted in Sheila Tobias et al. (eds.), *Cornell
Conference on Women*, Part 7, "The Black Woman in America" (Ithaca,
N.Y.: Cornell University, 1969), mimeographed, p. 18.
[13] Shirley Chisholm, "I'd Rather Be Black Than Be Female," *McCall's*,
Vol. 97, No. 11 (August 1970), p. 6.
[14] O'Neill, p. 10.

there isn't any movement ever going to be as powerful as the civil rights movement. Women haven't been denied their God-given rights. I've been free to do what I want to do. It's because a woman looked up to the man. But also, civil rights had love. With the women, they're fighting over each other. The minute you go in there you can feel it. We've got to have love and they don't have it in there.[15]

Another view is expressed by Sedwick and Williams in *The Black Scholar*. They advocate passage and note that many black organizations have gone on record as being pro-ERA. Among them: the NAACP, the National Council of Negro Women, the Coalition of Black Trade Unionists, the National Association of Negro Business and Professional Women's Clubs, and the National Black Feminist Organization, as well as many unions with large black memberships. They hold that "anti-ERA forces are trying to discourage black participation by saying that it is a 'white elitist movement' with no benefits for black women" and counter that "each gain for black women's rights is a gain for the black liberation movement. . . ." [16] Perhaps the majority of black women agree with Bolden: they do not trust white women enough to identify with women's liberation. Still, they will join in the ERA effort.

Implications for Personnel Practitioners

The evidence presented here suggests that personnel managers must continue to be alert to respect the rights of protected groups—minorities and women—and to recognize their special vulnerability as workers and prospective workers. It is easy to imagine a black woman with divided

[15] Nancy Seifer, *Nobody Speaks for Me! Self-Portraits of American Working Class Women* (New York: Simon and Schuster/Touchstone, 1976), p. 171.
[16] Cathy Sedwick and Reba Williams, "Black Women and the Equal Rights Amendment," *The Black Scholar*, Vol. 7, No. 9 (July–August 1976), pp. 24–29, p. 28.

loyalties: she is under pressure from black men and women to be active in civil rights and under pressure from white women and some black women to be loyal first and foremost to the women's cause. Add to that the burden of loneliness many black women feel because of the scarcity of black men. The conflicts must be substantial. But minority women, for all their troubles, have an independence and strength that many white women lack.

Pearl Gore Dansby, head of the department of psychology at Tennessee State University, has analyzed the phenomenon of "black pride" or, as she says, what some call "black arrogance." Reviewing studies of self-image among black people, she notes that before the 1960s there was clear evidence that many suffered from low self-esteem and high self-hatred. One example is that, for generations, black children preferred white dolls. Since the mid-1960s, Dansby notes, there have indeed been signs that black people are becoming self-conscious and proud of their blackness: this is a fact and not a fantasy. But she adds a cautionary note: "The brainwashing of generations cannot be erased in a decade, even in a young population. To be sure, evidence of self-hate, self-pity, and some identification with white values remained." [17] Other researchers are as skeptical of the self-image studies as they are of generalizations about "matriarchy" in black families. Studies involving dolls are suspect, they note, since in the 1960s black dolls were neither readily available in stores nor advertised on television. The few dolls that were available were mainly kerchief heads with red lips.

What specific counsel can be given? It seems that absolutely equal treatment will be difficult to achieve. The personnel practitioner who interacts with someone of her own background may immediately find shared beliefs and easy communication. This may not prove to be the case when

[17] Pearl Gore Dansby, "Black Pride in the Seventies: Fact or Fantasy?" in Reginald L. Jones (ed.), *Black Psychology* (New York: Harper & Row, 1972), pp. 145–155, p. 154.

she deals with a person very different from herself—say, a white male from a wealthy family. Misunderstandings arise: the two are trying to shout across a chasm of differences. To change the metaphor, they sometimes find that, despite goodwill, they are ships passing in the night.

Caution should also be exercised with job referrals. One personnel officer still recalls (with a certain bitterness) how she worked extra hard to help a black woman find an appropriate post. She found herself embroiled in a grievance so drawn-out, exhausting, and humiliating that she fervently wished she had never yielded to her original impulse. She believes to this day that she was set up, quoted absolutely incorrectly, and accused of being racist on grounds that were absolutely fabricated. All she can take comfort from is that the experience was educational.

The personnel practitioner should be on guard against the worst offense against any protected group: permitting the company to say it is acting affirmatively when it isn't. Hall notes that some companies are transferring minority staff members and/or women to jobs, formerly held by white males, that are neither promotions nor shifts desired by the employees. She cites the attempt to move women from light assembly or packing positions into jobs such as forklift truckdrivers and heavy machine operators. In both cases, she reports, employees resisted. Hall labels this a bad translation of affirmative action into reclassification or lateral transfer.[18]

Another pitfall to avoid is the exaggeration of progress. Nothing engenders cynicism among women employees faster than hearing managers boast of a "50 percent increase in the representation of women in the shipping department" when there were 20 workers there before, of whom one was a female, and now (flourish of trumpets!) there are two. Similarly, management should take pains to present

[18] Francine S. Hall, "Gaining EEO Compliance with a Stable Workforce," *Personnel Journal*, Vol. 56, No. 9 (September 1977), pp. 454–457, p. 454.

full statistics. Bragging that 17 new "minority and women executives" have been hired may not be well received by black women if there is in truth only one minority person in the group. And that one is a man.

In reporting progress to clients or current or prospective employees, companies are wiser to err by giving too much information than to mislead by giving too little. If 10 new minority managers are hired (in fact, desperately sought out because 20 left the outfit in one quarter), it is only fair to mention both the new hires and the fact that they bring the total to *whatever* it is.

Another practice to be avoided is the gerrymandering of job titles to mask the underrepresentation of women and/or minorities at high rungs of career ladders. It is, if not illegal, surely against the spirit of the law; more compelling, it is clearly unethical. An example from industry provided by attorney Robert S. Smith is shown below:

> *Example A:* Administrative assistant
> Executive secretary
> Junior secretary
> Stenographer
> Typist
> File clerk
> Clerk
> Mail clerk

Industrial organizations can group their titles by salary, career opportunity, or job content. The titles in Example A, above, do not have any of those characteristics in common. Indeed, reporting on the overall characteristics of that group by sex and race would suggest that women of all races and minority men were represented fairly evenly. A closer inspection of the incumbents by title, sex, and race shows that they are not. In the mail room, virtually all are minority males; in the clerical jobs, white females. The administrative assistants? Who can it be at that exempt and well-paid level? Who, indeed. And who is left out?

> *Example B:* Tool maker
> Machine operator A
> Machinist
> Machine helper
> Machine operator B
> Maintenance crew leader,
>   machine and tool area
> Janitor/custodian
> Restroom attendant

Example B is a grouping hard to justify as truly representing comparable salary levels, career opportunities, or job content. Women are represented only in the bottom two categories; no minority men can be found in the skilled trade categories.

> *Example C:* Professor
> Associate professor
> Assistant professor
> Instructor
> Lecturer
> Teaching assistant

The grouping in Example C, from academic life, masks the absence of women and minorities from the jobs on the tenure ladder, which begins in fact at the instructor level. Including lecturer in the grouping is misleading because it is a part-time position that does not lead to a professorship, which calls for research and scholarly publication. Including the teaching assistants is similarly unfair, since their duties sometimes just include correcting papers 15 hours a week; they are graduate students. The last two jobs are often held by women.

One teaching assistant at a university in Pennsylvania says that, as a graduate student, she not only graded papers but had a part-time job in central administration as well. Once she looked up the compliance reports at her institution and at first thought the authors were dreaming when they mentioned among the minorities and women two students and two faculty members in her department plus two employees in administration. Then she looked more closely and found that they had in fact counted her six times: once as a minority student, once as a woman student, once as a minority faculty member, once as a woman faculty member, and once each as a minority administrator and woman administrator.

The catalog of don'ts includes many other illegal acts and unethical practices. Perhaps almost as important, at least in terms of encouraging goodwill between the sexes in the workplace, is the avoidance of obvious discourtesies. A personnel practitioner reports that she was invited to make a presentation at a management club, one that had finally decided to open its doors to women. Indeed, she was to be the first woman speaker the club ever had.

In her presentation she alluded to the problems of minority women, explaining the nature of the double protection black women have and defending it as sorely needed and richly deserved. In conclusion, she urged those present to be sensitive to the problems that women of all races encounter in formerly all-male settings. After she resumed her place at the head table, the next speaker, a visitor from the club's regional office, gave his presentation. His theme was that local chapters must plan their meetings carefully and encourage all current members to recruit new people. He held up a box directly in the face of the previous speaker and said, "Your programs should be like what's in this box—something everyone will love and be dying to get into." He opened the box slowly, prolonging the suspense. The previous speaker watched with a smile; it had flashed through her mind that the organization might, as women's clubs sometimes do, be giving her a present.

But the contents that he held high in the air turned out to be a gigantic brassiere. The men in the lecture room laughed heartily, but the women didn't know where to look. And the speaker herself was frozen with embarrassment and dismay. Recounting that mortifying experience the next day in the office, the speaker found that her colleagues' reactions varied enormously. A male co-worker said he guessed she must be losing her sense of humor. A white woman said she should have whipped out her matches and set that bra on fire. Another white woman disagreed because, although the men would have loved that, the women would have been even more uncomfortable. Her view was that all women have trouble enough with that "stupid bra-burner image."

A black colleague gave the speaker the most food for thought. "I don't know why you white women run around worrying about images," she said. "Why waste your time with those jocks? Who cares about changing men's attitudes? I don't give a damn whether they like us or not. They just better respect our rights at work. Or they'll be sorry."

We have a message for George Meany!
We have a message for Leonard
Woodcock! We have a message for
Frank Fitzsimmons! You can tell them
we didn't come here to swap recipes.
—Myra Wolfgang, union vice president,
at the founding meeting of the Coalition
of Labor Union Women (CLUW) [1]

7

The Public Sector,
The Private Employer,
and Women's
Organizations

WOMEN workers are, in fact, beginning to band together to
take action. The groups are few in comparison with the
numbers of women who are working either as public servants or in the private sector. The 1980s will bring the answer as to whether women will ever, as a group, be as pow-

[1] Reported in Patsy Sims, "After Hectic Weekend, the CLUW Gives
Birth," *Philadelphia Inquirer*, March 25, 1974, pp. 7–8.

erful as their numbers suggest they could be. In this chapter we will consider the situation of women employed by the government versus that of women in private business and industry; we will also examine the growth of organization among women and the forms it is taking, from associations of clerical workers through integrated labor unions to the CLUW.

Women in Public Service

Women who work for the government can, theoretically, choose from the widest possible range of jobs, since that sector includes nearly all the occupations in private business and some additional jobs as well. Public service work includes posts to which individuals are appointed or elected and those for which candidates compete through the civil service system.

Women comprise a very small proportion of those citizens elected or appointed to public office, as shown in Table 16. The more prestigious the office, the fewer the women. A study of individual biographies shows that nearly half of all women who have ever served in Congress have been related to a previous officeholder. They, like the Honorable Muriel Humphrey and Honorable Margaret Chase Smith, were appointed (and sometimes later elected) to take the place of a husband or father. A similar study of women in top management posts in business might show that they too count among their ranks many who had access to their positions because of the powerful males to whom they were related by birth or marriage.

Excluded from Table 16 is the category of volunteer campaign worker, where women may be best represented. The duties of that post include stuffing envelopes, knocking on doors, and holding neighborhood "coffees" for candidates. One 1973 study of political participation suggested that a single event in a woman's life more than any other affected her participation in political activity, from running

Table 16. Women in public office, 1975–1976.

Office	Total Number	Number Women	Percent Women
Cabinet member	—	1	—
U.S. Senator	100	—	—
Member, House of Representatives	435	19	4
Federal judge	675	8	1
State governor	50	1	2
Lieutenant governor	50	3	6
State secretary	50	11	22
State cabinet member	1,300*	139	10
State legislature member	7,561	610	9
County commissioner	17,000*	456	2.5
Mayor or town council member	136,000*	5,947	5
School board member	96,560	11,000	11

Source: Adapted from *To Form a More Perfect Union: Justice for American Women*, report of the National Commission on the Observance of International Women's Year (Washington, D.C.: U.S. Government Printing Office, 1976), p. 341.
* Estimated.

for office herself to supporting others' campaigns to voting itself. The event: having a baby. The fact of motherhood has a permanent effect on women's political behavior such that women's level of participation, which is at least equal to men's until they bear children, never again catches up.[2]

Whatever the reason, women are ill-represented in appointive or elective office. They are better represented in those public service jobs where individual merit is said to be the determining factor. Indeed, it can be said that women workers encounter fewer personnel problems (and present fewer to practitioners) in the civil service than they do in the private sector.

Twenty percent of all American workers are employed by federal, state, and local governments.[3] Government is the nation's largest employer and, it is said, the most progressive.[4] Clara Barton believed herself to be the first woman employee of the government appointed on the same basis as a man. She was hired by the U.S. Patent Office in 1854 as a clerk-copyist and found herself to be the victim of intense discrimination. As she went into work, the men would line up in the halls to stare, blow smoke in her face, spit tobacco juice, make catcalls, and harass her with obnoxious remarks. After seven years, she left the federal service for a more womanly job as a nurse.[5]

Abraham Lincoln appointed a feminist, General Francis Elias Spinner, to the post of Treasurer of the United States. It was Spinner who set out to distribute the jobs equitably among candidates rather than treating them as political plums. Spinner appointed Mrs. Sophia Holmes as janitress in his department, the first official appointment ever con-

[2] Naomi B. Lynn and Cornelia Butler Flora, "Motherhood and Political Participation: The Changing Sense of Self," *Journal of Political and Military Sociology*, Vol. 1 (Spring 1973), 91–103.
[3] Rosabeth Moss Kanter, *Men and Women of the Corporation* (New York: Basic Books, 1977), p. 15.
[4] Jayne B. Spain, "Women in Government and Affirmative Action," in Dorothy Jongeward and Dru Scott (eds.), *Affirmative Action for Women: A Practical Guide* (Reading, Mass.: Addison-Wesley, 1974), pp. 71–89, p. 74.
[5] Ross K. Baker, "Entry of Women into Federal Job World—at a Price," *Smithsonian Magazine*, Vol. 8, No. 4 (July 1977), pp. 82–87.

ferred on a black woman. Mrs. Holmes was the widow of a black soldier (a former slave) who was killed in the Battle of Bull Run. She had been working in the department unofficially at a salary of $15 a month. One day she came upon no less than $200,000 in bills that had, by error, been thrown into the wastebasket. Mrs. Holmes stood guard over the money far into the night until Spinner made his rounds; then she turned the bills over to him. As a reward, she was officially appointed at $55 a month. This was a generous increase, but still far below the wage paid to any male employee.[6]

The Civil Service Act of 1883 created the Civil Service Commission and decreed that employment would be regulated by competitive examinations, open to all Americans. That summer, Mary Francis Hoyt, a Vassar graduate, was among the candidates taking the first civil service examination; she received the highest mark given on that first test. Hoyt's name went to the head of the list. The first appointment made from the list went to a man (Hoyt was out of town at the time), but seven days later she was in fact appointed.[7] The system of appointment on merit appeared to be to women's advantage; their numbers increased. In 1972 Patricia Marshall reported that the government was well ahead of private industry in terms of the proportion of women employees in professional and technical posts. Of the white women civil servants, 43 percent were in those high-level jobs and of black women, 34 percent. In private industry, only 8 percent of the white women were so classified and only 2 percent of the black women.[8]

But a number of problems remained. Executive Order 11375 and subsequent administrative actions opened opportunities to women; but as Janice Mendenhall reports, after eight years there was little change. (See Table 17.)

In seeking to explain the absence of women from the high-level grades, Mendenhall examines the assumptions

[6] Baker, p. 86.

[7] Spain, p. 81.

[8] Patricia Marshall, "Women at Work," *Manpower* (U.S. Department of Labor), Vol. 4, No. 6 (June 1972).

Table 17. White collar federal
employees, by sex and rank.

Rank	*Percent Women*	
	1967	*1975*
GS 1 to 6	73	72
GS 7 to 11	25	32
GS 12 to 15	5	7
GS 16 to 18	2	3
All ranks	43	42

Source: Adapted from Janice
Mendenhall, "Career Women in
the Federal Government," paper
presented to the American Society
for Public Administration, Atlanta,
Ga., March 30, 1977, mimeographed, p. 1.

that women have less service, lower performance ratings,
and less education than their male counterparts. She cites
studies that suggest strongly that those assumptions are absolutely false. Especially convincing are her data on educational level. It appears that when men and women federal
employees have the same amount of education, the men are
employed at least one grade group higher than the women.
For example, men holding a bachelor's degree are as a
group between GS 9 and GS 11. Women with that degree
are between GS 5 and GS 8.[9]

Another problem in the federal service appears to be the
overall underrepresentation of women. Women as a group
hold 42 percent of federal white collar jobs but only 34
percent of all federal jobs. Table 18 shows that women still
have not regained the proportion of government jobs they
held during World War II.

Chambers reports that until 1961 government agencies
were permitted to fill job openings by requesting candi-

[9] Janice Mendenhall, "Career Women in the Federal Government,"
paper presented to the American Society for Public Administration, Atlanta, Ga., March 30, 1977, mimeographed, p. 5.

Table 18. Women in the
federal service.

Date	Women as Percent of Federal Workforce
1939	19
1944	37
1947	24
1952	25
1968	34
1970	33
1972	34
1973	34

Source: Angela Chambers,
"Changes in the Federal Ser-
vice," lecture presented at
Cornell University, New York
State School of Industrial and
Labor Relations, Ithaca, N.Y.,
October 12, 1977, Chart A.

dates from a male or female register without stating any
reasons for their preferences. In 1962, at the request of the
President's Commission on the Status of Women, chaired
by Eleanor Roosevelt, the Civil Service Commission began
to require that agencies explain why they wanted to consider candidates of only one sex. Before that time, requests
had run 56 percent for the male registry only, 17 percent for
the female registry only, and 27 percent for both. (Of all the
job requests, 29 percent had been for the male list; of the
jobs at the GS 13–15 level, 94 percent of the requests had
been for the male list.)

After the Civil Service Commission acted, single-sex
requests dwindled to less than 1 percent. What reasons had
agencies given for asking to see only the women's list?
Work was "monotonous," "detailed," "repetitious"; the
post offered "only limited advancement opportunities."
Samples of the reasons given for a request to see only the
male register: "arduous and hazardous duties," "travel,"
"rotating assignments," "bad location," "contact with pub-

lic." All those reasons were declared invalid, and in 1962 Attorney General Robert Kennedy ruled that only agencies seeking to fill jobs requiring carrying a gun or certain custodial positions could request single-sex registries.[10]

Despite that ruling, a number of problems still plague women employed by the government. Although women are inching up from the bottom six grades to the next five, there are still few at the top levels compared with the numbers of men there. Little attention has been focused on the provision of career ladders for clerical workers and on the dearth of women in the "supergrades," those off the top of the career ladders of general service classifications. In a January 1978 article entitled "All the President's Women," Blythe Babyak observed: "In 200 years of the United States' history, only five women have been appointed to Cabinet posts, and two of them are serving in the current Cabinet. In the last administration, only 5 percent of the top presidential appointees were women; now 12 percent of these coveted jobs are held by women." [11]

At the state level, women civil servants are faced with many of the same problems found at the federal level. A pervasive problem, according to a study undertaken by Diane Steinberg, a student intern in the New York State legislature, is that comparable jobs are classified quite differently.[12] After a study of job titles, she concluded that social worker (entry level GS 14) is comparable to probation officer (entry level GS 17); psychiatric attendant (GS 5) is comparable to corrections officer (GS 14); and principal secretary (GS 12) is comparable to administrative assistant (GS 18). In each case, she notes, the lower-rated job is held primarily by women; the higher-rated job, by men.

[10] Angela Chambers, "Changes in the Federal Service," lecture presented at Cornell University, New York State School of Industrial and Labor Relations, Ithaca, N.Y., October 12, 1977.

[11] Blythe Babyak, "All the President's Women," *New York Times Magazine*, January 22, 1978, p. 11.

[12] Diane B. Steinberg, "Reform of the New York State Civil Service," testimony prepared under the auspices of the office of Lieutenant Governor Mary Ann Krupsak and included in the public record of hearings held May 1977, mimeographed.

Steinberg found three additional practices that barred the progress of women up the career ladders: (1) the fact that a candidate must have a bachelor's degree in order to take the Professional Careers Test; (2) evidence that the "rule of three" (that appointing authorities must choose among the top three scorers on tests) is being subverted; and (3) the preferential treatment given to veterans of military service.

In recognition of the first problem, Steinberg notes that the position of administrative aide was created in 1975 to serve as a bridge between the clerical and professional ranks; expertise is considered as valid a qualification for the position as a college degree. Staff members at the GS 7 level and above were qualified to take the examination for administrative aide; between 2,000 and 3,000 have passed the test. But as of June 1977, only 14 appointments have been made. Some state systems are better than New York's in terms of the "rule of three." Steinberg cites the Illinois system of block scoring, which divides applicants into four groups according to their scores: the "well qualified" top 25 percent; the "qualified" 30 percent; the "minimally qualified" 40 percent; and the "ineligible" bottom 5 percent. Those in the top block must be hired before the next block can be certified.

In the matter of veterans' preference, Steinberg concludes that the system is an institutionalized barrier to women's progress in that women have traditionally had a much lower participation rate in the military than men have. A Wisconsin study demonstrated that the 10-point benefit to a disabled veteran (one who has at least a 10 percent disability) resulted in a marked increase in rank; a 5-point benefit to a nondisabled veteran resulted in a very slight increase in rank; and absence of veterans' credit brought about a marked decrease in rank. The impact of veterans' preference is accentuated in the upper-level professional positions, according to additional data gathered by the Wisconsin team. The chances of a nonveteran obtaining a top management job in state service are therefore exceedingly and unfairly slim.

In short, the evidence suggests that neither the federal government nor state governments can be considered model affirmative action employers. Although their record is better in many respects than the one earned by private employers, it seems that neither appointment to the civil service nor promotion within it is based entirely on merit.

The Private Sector

An executive guidebook on compliance with EEO legislation suggests that corporate policymakers do not fully appreciate the risks they run by oversight. Although the press coverage has suggested that only major companies have been the targets of lawsuits, subject to judgments of millions of dollars because of noncompliance, "thousands of smaller companies dependent on government contracts have learned too late that government enforcement falls equally on large and small." [13]

It is clear that big companies have suffered. The Corning Glass Works paid $500,000 in back pay to women employees; Standard Oil of New Jersey paid $775,000 to the widow of an employee who was allegedly discriminated against because of his age; and AT&T paid $15 million in back wages to 15,000 women and minority group men and an additional $23 million in raises to 36,000 employees. The guidebook suggests to managers that there are warning signals of a potential lawsuit. Among them:

1. A petition to management from minority or female employees requesting redress.
2. A complaint by an individual that he or she has been passed over for promotion.
3. Complaints to the union.
4. Formation of a minority or women's group within the organization.

[13] Management/Employee Relations Counsel and Ronald M. Green, *Equal Employment Opportunity: An Executive's Guide to Compliance* (New York: Hill & Knowlton, n.d.), pp. 2, 16.

5. Action taken against another company in the industry or in the same geographic area.

Virtually all these warning signs have been in evidence in the federal government. But public servants have recourse to fewer legal remedies than do employees of private businesses.

The differences in corporate response to one of these signals—a petition from a women's committee—illustrate, in some respects, the vulnerability of management. At the American Broadcasting Company in 1972, a group of women employees presented management with a petition outlining two major problems: (1) the way women as a group were presented in network programs and (2) the status of women employees within the company. Management responded by setting up a meeting between the petitioners and the president of the network. At that meeting the president and other top managers listened attentively to the evidence the employees presented and agreed, after subsequent meetings, to take major steps to change the situation. Management drew up an affirmative action plan that included internal job posting among other efforts to make possible advancement of the women employees.

Today the women's committee at ABC still maintains open channels of communication with management. Members find that they must work to resolve certain problems before they can expect top management to act. One member notes that many women staff members have "too circumscribed a fantasy life" in terms of their own potential for serious careers in broadcasting. So the group has set up a series of luncheon meetings at which women who have progressed to middle management in various departments speak to the others and answer their questions about the training needed for high-level jobs, the nature of the demands once responsible jobs have been gained, and other issues related to the advancement of women. The women's committee believes that some levels of management are complacent about the progress being made and that more work needs to be done. Nevertheless, the committee anticipates approaching the problems without the help of the law.[14]

The National Broadcasting Company, in contrast, responded to a similar petition from its women employees by delaying four months. The answer finally came in the form of a presentation by middle managers that essentially defended the network against the charges the women had levied. Particularly galling to the women was a slide show that purported to demonstrate how well women as a group were portrayed on network shows. In fact, management had misunderstood the nature of the women's complaint—some of the shows used as evidence of "good image" were precisely the ones the women employees had found offensive. The women's committee, despairing of being heard, on the issue of either the image on the shows or of the status of women in the network's employ, filed a lawsuit and won $2 million.

A similar effort by a woman's group in private industry—at Procter & Gamble Co.—failed, not because of the nature of management's response but because of internal dissent. The committee was composed of women professionals and of clerical workers. Their aims proved to be too diverse; the group was unable to agree on the nature of its requests to management. But as we have seen, internal action can bring about change if there are managers willing to listen and empowered to act.

Women Organizing for Change

Some women workers see unionization as a mixed blessing. Like management, they are uneasy about the introduction of regularized collective bargaining, contract negotiations, and so forth. Part of the reason for this "womanly

[14] Robin Forst and Shelly Page, "Portents of Change in Unions," lecture presented at Cornell University, New York State of Industrial & Labor Relations, Ithaca, N.Y., October 10, 1977.

resistance" is the fact that trade unions, until quite recently, have not had a good record on women's issues. Unions have not, in general, made major efforts to organize women workers. Women members complain that their dues are going to support the men's causes and that unions sometimes ally with management in perpetuating practices that maintain the status quo for women.[15]

Although women make up over half the population and two-fifths of the workforce, they comprise only a fifth of the labor union membership. Put another way, only 13 percent of all woman workers are members of unions. An even lower proportion are union leaders—even in predominantly female unions. Only 5 percent of union leaders are women, while 6 percent of top managers are women. So it is said by some that management is a little more likely to welcome women to its ranks than big labor is.

A review of the history of women unionists shows that most of the organization has taken place in the needle trades. There, originally, women formed their own unions because they could not gain admission to the men's. Even after unions opened their doors to women, however, few women workers went in.

Why haven't women joined unions with the enthusiasm that men have? Seven reasons have been advanced:

1. The image of unions is male; women do not feel comfortable in smoke-filled halls. Some say they find the organizations too "hoody" for their tastes.

2. Women workers, of whom a third are part-time, have no real commitment to the job and therefore no compelling reason to join a union to bring about changes in conditions.

3. The husbands of women workers, especially those in blue collar jobs, won't permit their wives to go to evening meetings and certainly not to be active as leaders, traveling away from home with groups of men.

---

[15] Gail Falk, "Sex Discrimination in the Trade Unions: Legal Resources for Change" in Jo Freeman (ed.), *Women: A Feminist Perspective* (Palo Alto, CA: Mayfield, 1975), pp. 254–276.

4. Women workers by and large have too many home responsibilities to take on the extra responsibility of membership, never mind leadership duties.

5. The unions do not want women workers as members enough to recruit them as aggressively as they do men. Although union leaders espouse equal pay for equal work, some still believe that no woman could ever do certain jobs as well as a man could.

6. Women workers see little advantage to joining organizations that seem to be as insensitive to women's problems as they believe management is—and as reluctant to take action to resolve them.

7. Most women workers are in occupations and industries where traditionally unions have not flourished. A prime example is the clerical worker.

Barbara Wertheimer illustrates the barriers to women's participation in unions with the case of Boston clerical workers. Women formed a group called Nine to Five to set about to change conditions for women secretaries and other clerical workers. After the initial organizing effort, the group decided that it would be better off if it were affiliated with a mainstream union. The women had to go to ten unions in the Boston area before they found one willing to finance the group's organizing drive and to admit its members on their own terms. One of their conditions was that they be allowed to keep their identification as "Nine to Fivers"; as a result, the group is now Local 925, part of a recognized AFL-CIO union.

Wertheimer counts the foundation of CLUW—the Coalition of Labor Union Women—as an important step toward the organization of women workers. Open only to trade unionists, CLUW sets about to bring changes in women's roles in their unions, in their participation in the political structure, in the passage of legislation important to working women, and in the organizing of unorganized women workers. CLUW was influential, Wertheimer reports, in the AFL-CIO reversal of its anti-ERA position. Such gains, she holds, suggest the potential power of women if they act collectively as trade unionists.[16]

Wertheimer points to the fact that the Communications Workers of America declared "equality for women" as a key bargaining issue for 1977. Although CLUW has a modest membership of only 5,000, she notes that the coalition is active through its 30 chapters on such issues as pregnancy disability, ERA, national health insurance, occupational health and safety, and improved child care. Full employment is a number one issue.

Within CLUW, a Task Force on Model Contract Clauses provides women trade unionists in a variety of unions with information and guidelines for negotiating clauses on maternity and parental leave, job posting, and other anti-discrimination clauses. Finally, Wertheimer notes that university and labor union education programs increasingly focus on subjects relating to union women. Just one example was the two-day conference on the theme of organizing white collar workers that was sponsored by the AFL-CIO in 1977.

Joyce D. Miller, international vice president of the Amalgamated Clothing and Textile Workers Union, is current president of CLUW. She is convinced that CLUW's success in fighting off attempts by outside radical groups to use it as an instrument for advancing their own agenda has left it well equipped to grow. Wertheimer shares the view that the growth potential of CLUW is tremendous but suggests the need to demonstrate "that the financial aid it receives from established unions is not stripping it of required independence." [17]

Other observers are less optimistic about CLUW, criticizing its posture as reformist, its membership policies as shortsighted and exclusionary, and its goals as narrow

---

[16] Barbara Mayer Wertheimer, *We Were There: The Story of Working Women in America* (New York: Pantheon Books, 1977), pp. 369–376.

[17] A. H. Raskin, "Growing Acceptance for the Coalition of Union Women," *The New York Times*, October 19, 1977, p. L-D3.

and ultimately self-defeating for women workers.[18] Only
time will tell which of the analysts is correct.

A recent report by a *Washington Post* columnist noted
that "3,000 women office workers have formed organizations in more than a dozen American cities, including Boston, Cleveland, Chicago, Dayton, New York, San Francisco,
and Detroit." Elizabeth Schneider, co-founder of Sixty
Words Per Minute, Washington, D.C., remarked that her
group is one of the newest: "It's strange that it has taken
Washington so long to catch on. You'd think it would be a
hotbed of activity, but perhaps federal employees feel they
are better paid than most office workers or are frightened
about their jobs. . . ."

In Cleveland, the Working Women Organizing Project
has reportedly won many cases from "changing desks
around to getting back pay and increases in salaries. . . .
When a woman was fired in Chicago for not getting coffee,
40 members picketed and protested. She was rehired." [19] In
San Francisco, Women Organized for Employment won a
ban on sex-segregated job listings in advertising by news-
papers and employment agencies.

In Chicago, Women Employed (WE) had won more than
$1.1 million in back pay awards. WE is the oldest of the new
office workers' organizations; it uses tactics ranging from
individual counseling to class-action lawsuits. But its main
function is to "solicit complaints from disgruntled office
workers and file charges with state or federal agencies."
WE relies heavily on street theater and uses the mass media
effectively. Following a recent dispute with Harris Trust &
Savings Bank in Chicago, WE awarded John L. Stephens
(senior vice president for employee relations) its Dubious
Achievement Award for doing "the least for equal opportunity this year." As WE presented him with the certificate,

[18] Annemarie Tröger, "The Coalition of Labor Union Women: Strategic
Hope, Tactical Despair," in Rosalyn Baxandall, Linda Gordon, and Susan
Reverby (eds.), *America's Working Women: A Documentary History, 1600
to the Present* (New York: Vintage Books, 1976), pp. 390–399.

[19] Myra MacPherson, "Secretaries Are Organizing: Take This Letter,
but First Put the Coffee On," *Ithaca (N.Y.) Journal*, March 10, 1978, p. 9.

TV cameras whirred. The organization has won many cases but has lost some as well, in part because of lack of support from traditional unions. That experience has left WE leaders "dubious about organized labor's interest in office workers." [20]

Many feel that the women's committee and ultimately the women's union is the only route to change for women workers. Others call for the inclusion of women in traditional unions, but only those that have demonstrated willingness to negotiate on women's issues, rather than bargaining such issues away before they get down to the "real business" of representing the majority of their membership.

The Federal Women's Program (FWP) is an inside effort to cleanse the civil service of some of the internal hindrances to women's progress outlined earlier in this chapter. It was established by the Civil Service Commission in 1967 to enhance the status of women in federal employment and to redress past inequities. Each government agency has a full-time FWP coordinator; each department has one employee released part-time to assist her. In 1968 women staff members formed a group called Federally Employed Women (FEW) to assist FWP from the outside, as it were. Unlike FWP, which operates with government funding, FEW can take political action, lobby, and protest. FEW found that, within a few months, it could indeed bring about change even in a slow-moving bureaucracy using what has proved to be its most powerful weapon to date: publicity. There are unions in government service—among them, the National Treasury Employees' Union—but they have not been any more helpful to women in the 1970s than the Patent Office men were to Clara Barton in the 1850s.

The woman worker who sets out to choose between the government and a private employer may find herself between a rock and a hard place. While there is more prestige in working in the private sector, there appears to be more

[20] Joann S. Lublin, "Secretaries' Revolt," *The Wall Street Journal*, February 24, 1978, p. 1.

protection of women's rights in public service, for all its problems. Should the woman worker seek to found a women's committee in either sector, she will find enormous problems within (in seeking to come to agreement with others on tactics and priorities) and without (in that management may well give the committee petitions short shrift).

Some women feel that the Equal Employment Opportunity Commission, with its backlog of 90,000 cases and its own history of being charged with discrimination, cannot be relied on to act either fast enough or fairly enough to right wrongs. Many women workers would not dream of seeking legal assistance for their work problems, which they attribute to a variety of malignant forces they could not dare to challenge. But a few do dare. They persevere in the face of management opposition and union indifference. They are the ones who brought about the judgments that cause managers in public service and in profit centers alike to think twice before they dismiss women's grievances as trivial.

It is tough when all the women are
secretaries and all the men are
lawyers.
—*Judy McCullough, co-founder of Nine
to Five, an organization of women office
workers* [1]

8

"Women's Work
Is Never Done"
—by Men

THE pervasive nature of sex segregation at work and the
narrow range of jobs held by women are factors that seem
certain to affect women's performance on the job. It is unlikely that women were destined by nature to perform a
restricted number of tasks while men were designed to do
everything else. Anthropologist Margaret Mead put her

[1] Cited in Myra MacPherson, "Secretaries Are Organizing: Take This
Letter, but First Put the Coffee On," *Ithaca (N.Y.) Journal*, March 10, 1978,
p. 9.

finger on the artificiality of this segregation when she noted that the designation of given tasks as "men's work" or "women's work" varies by culture. In one tribe, basket weaving is seen as work for women; in another, a task for men. Always and everywhere, she notes, no matter what the task is, if men do it, it is seen as more important than if women do it.

So long as women are seen as fit for (and prepare themselves for) only certain lines of work, personnel managers will be plagued by problems of women workers who find themselves in jobs to which they are not suited. The aim of this chapter is to consider the extent of job segregation at the blue collar and service level, in clerical work and saleswork, and at the professional and managerial level. As we shall see, at each level men's work and women's work are sharply differentiated and women are crowded into a handful of jobs.

In 1970 half the women workers in this country (a fifth of the total workforce) were concentrated in seventeen occupations. Half the men were distributed among 63 occupations.[2] This breakdown reflects only work done for pay. Excluded is the one job for which all women are seen as fitted from birth: houseworker, an occupation that is more than 99 percent segregated. Also excluded is community volunteer, another job that is dominated by women, but to a lesser extent than houseworker is. It is clear that keeping house or running a Kiwanis paper drive or a Girl Scout cookie campaign is not *leisure* activity, but for this purpose it shall not be considered work because it is not paid. (The exclusion of housewife and community volunteer from the definition of work places a great many women at a disadvantage when they seek to return to the paid workforce. Older women find that the expertise they have developed at home and in the community is discounted as though it were time off.)

[2] Rosabeth Moss Kanter, *Men and Women of the Corporation* (New York: Basic Books, 1977), p. 16.

The definition of work is not of mere academic interest. On October 16, 1977, women from the Seneca Falls area in New York State gathered to discuss issues with delegates who would be attending the National Women's Conference in Houston in November. One speaker noted that a common concern was the plight of the housewife with little legal protection. This prompted a heated exchange in the *Rochester (N.Y.) Times Union* of November 10, 1977, and November 22, 1977. One writer noted:

> When [that speaker said] "Women's work is not considered real work," she did not speak for me and the women who prefer to choose the traditional role of a woman in a traditional family. (That's *real* work!) . . .

To which another person who had been present responded:

> [The previous writer] takes issue with the statement "women's work is not considered real work." Isn't she aware that often our laws do not recognize it as "real work" and do not take it into consideration? Society classifies her as a parasite and [she finds herself] without the equity rights she has earned. . . .

The first writer argues that she is working hard as a housewife, burning calories, doing an important job, and certainly not lounging around. The second, while conceding that, points out that the activity is not rewarded as actual participation in the workforce is—through legal protection, social security benefits, and so forth. It seems that they almost *seek* to misunderstand one another. A housewife cannot be expected to respond favorably to being called a "parasite," even if the intent is not to hurt her feelings but to point out a legal reality.

Even if we narrow the definition of work to jobs done for pay, problems arise in grouping the 23,000 listings in the *Dictionary of Occupational Titles* in any way other than the categories designated by the Bureau of Labor Statistics (from officials/administrators down to service/maintenance). Kanter defines white collar work by implication as the tasks involved in "operating the administrative machines that run large organizations." [3] Jean Boyce differentiates between white collar work (that of processing components dealing with goods and services) and blue collar labor (that having to do with manufacturing but not contact with the client for whom a product is manufactured) and inserts a new category of "pink collar work" between the two. Pink collar jobs, as she defines them, are those that provide the service connection between the blue collar workers (who are directed by the white collarites) and the client.[4] A different view is provided by Louise Kapp Howe, author of *Pink Collar Workers*, who defines the pink collar worker as the person who does a job mostly done by women.

Problems arise when we try to classify jobs in terms of the clothing worn by the jobholders. Many sociologists have noted that working-class people wear fancier clothing than that chosen by the elite. This is particularly apparent at a high-prestige university where wealthy students of both sexes affect the garb once associated with the working class—work boots, painter's overalls, and a workshirt that indeed is blue and has a blue collar.

Of course "collar color" is not always linked with income. Trade union leader Addie Wyatt reported that in 1941, when she was 17, she applied for an office job at Armour and Company, Chicago. She was hired, not in the office but on the line in the factory, filling cans with stew. She was disappointed but kept hoping she would be transferred to the office—until she found she earned more money than office workers. Her co-workers explained that they belonged to a union; the clerical workers didn't.

Sociologists like to consider how it should be that a janitor in a grade school who goes back to college to be certified as a teacher and then is appointed in the same

[3] Kanter, p. 15.
[4] Jean Boyce, cited in *Dialogue: A Newsletter for Cornell Women at Work*, Vol. 4, No. 11 (November 30, 1977), p. 11.

grade school can earn a lower salary than he did before. Feminist Dorothy Haener, international representative of the United Auto Workers, asks: "Where is it written that an industrial nurse should be paid less than a millwright or an electrician? When you compare educational backgrounds and the skills used, you really have to question the pay rates. . . . In most factories the secretary earns less than the floor sweeper." [5]

Women seldom have those jobs as floor sweepers. However, according to a representative of the New York State Department of Labor, last year a woman was placed in a public job in Albany as a sweeper, where she earned $20,000 a year counting overtime pay. She didn't last long—in part because her husband did not want her to continue working there.

Blue Collar Jobs

The largest category of women workers to be considered here is comprised of those we shall designate as blue collar: factory workers, those in domestic service in private households, service workers, and those who work on farms. Of the 32 million women working in 1973, 40 percent were in these occupations, as shown in Table 19. The category of service workers includes nearly 2.5 million in food service: more than a million waitresses and counter and fountain workers. There are also 1.4 million in health service jobs as nursing aides, orderlies, practical nurses, and dental assistants. Other large categories in this group: 460,000 hairdressers and 700,000 building cleaners. The semiskilled category ("operatives") includes sewers and stitchers and those who do assembly, packing, wrapping, and checking in factories.

[5] *To Form a More Perfect Union: Justice for American Women,* report of the National Commission on the Observance of International Women's Year (Washington, D.C.: U.S. Government Printing Office, 1976), p. 65.

Table 19. Women in blue collar jobs, 1973.

Major Occupational Group	Number (in millions)	Percent of Total Female Workforce
Service workers	5.7	18
Semiskilled workers	4.5	14
Household workers	1.3	4
Farm workers	.5	1.5
Others	.8	3
	12.8	40

Source: Adapted from *1975 Handbook on Women Workers* (Washington, D.C.: U.S. Department of Labor, 1975), p. 100.

Blue collar workers are the least studied of any workers in American life. Barbara Garson has written about factory operatives. Her interest was sparked by the idea that people who do assembly work, repeating the same task over and over, must find small routines to give the work the interest it seems to lack. Indeed, she found a worker who loved the soft, sensuous colors in the tuna fish she cleaned:

> . . . the reds and the whites and the purples, and the most exciting thing is the dark meat. It comes in streaks. It's red-brown. And you have to pull it out with your knife. . . . It's crumbly and dark red and moist like earth. You're supposed to put the cat food on the belt as you finish each loin. But I hold it out to make as big a pile of dark meat as I can. . . .[6]

The situation of waitresses was first investigated by William Foote Whyte in a pioneering article called "The Social Structure of a Restaurant." Whyte found a hitherto unnoticed problem in male/female relations at work. This piece of information was instantly recognized by food service workers as a classic case—something everybody always sort of knew but somehow never acted upon. The restaurant Whyte observed was having personnel problems

[6] Barbara Garson, *All the Livelong Day: The Meaning and Demeaning of Routine Work* (New York: Penguin Books, 1975), p. 24.

at the juncture where the waitress called the orders to the cook. Whyte observed that men didn't like to take orders from women, especially women they outranked. A solution was devised. A barrier was erected between the chef and the waitresses, who were instructed to write down their orders.[7]

More recent work on the occupation of waitresses has been undertaken by two anthropologists, the one a professor, James Spradley, and the other his student, Brenda Mann. Mann based her Ph.D. dissertation on her work as a cocktail waitress in a college bar. Their joint book is a substantial contribution to the understanding of male/female problems at work. They examine such issues as the status gap between bartenders and waitresses, employees' territoriality, and the curious joking relationship that a cocktail waitress maintains with favored clients.[8]

Louise Kapp Howe has likewise gone behind the scenes to study waitresses who are old-timers. She observes that the occupation is a seductive one for young women, who seldom imagine that it will be a full-time career. Its advantages as stopgap work are apparent in that there are few jobs where the time between doing the work and getting the pay is so satisfactorily short. Right after the meal, the waitresses divide up the tips.[9] This is a clear advantage to the young woman, for whom the sums are comparatively big, given her experience. What is not clear to the young woman is that her older, experienced co-worker is not any further up a career ladder. The job is absolutely dead end. Raises are practically unheard of. Even if the basic salary were raised, the take-home pay would be little affected, since salary forms such a small part of earnings.

The occupation of farm worker, though a dwindling one

[7] William Foote Whyte, "The Social Structure of a Restaurant," *American Journal of Sociology*, Vol. 54, No. 4 (January 1949), pp. 302–310.

[8] James Spradley and Brenda Mann, *The Cocktail Waitress: Woman's Work in a Man's World* (New York: John Wiley & Sons, 1975).

[9] Louise Kapp Howe, *Pink Collar Workers: Inside the World of Women's Work* (New York: G. P. Putnam's Sons, 1977).

according to the Census figures, is a sore point for two reasons. The first is that migrant workers number among them many women and children who are at least as exploited as male workers: "The migrant mother doesn't even understand the notion of staying at home and taking care of her children. . . . When the husband goes out, the entire family joins him working—and day care for the migrant mother is a fruit box in the field for the baby." [10]

A second problem for women who work on farms is their lack of legal protection. Mary Heath of Cody, Nebraska, worked alongside her husband on their 3,395-acre farm taking care of the cattle, helping with haying, and raising hogs on the side. In 1974, when her husband died, she learned she would have to pay a $25,000 inheritance tax, which means she may have to sell the farm. If she had died first, her husband would not have had to pay any inheritance tax on their joint property. [11]

Domestic work is the least regulated of any blue collar category. This worker is quite likely to be beyond middle years and to be a member of a minority group. More than a fifth of minority women aged 35 and older are in domestic service compared with only 6 percent of black women aged 16 to 34. In contrast, of white women workers, 3 percent of each age group are domestics. Domestic workers have been covered by the minimum wage since 1974, with the extension of the Fair Labor Standards Act. According to the Women's Bureau, in 1973 the year-round full-time domestic worker earned a median annual wage of $2,069.

What, then, do these workers have in common? It can be seen that there are comparatively short training periods for certain blue collar occupations, such as waitressing and working as a domestic. For waitresses, this is offset by a comparatively high entry-level pay. In each category, year-round full-time women employees earn less than men, with

---

[10] "Rural Women, with 'Stories to Tell,' Gather in Capital," *The New York Times*, February 25, 1978, p. 6.

[11] *To Form a More Perfect Union: Justice for American Women*, p. 13.

women factory operatives earning 56.4 percent and service workers 57.8 percent of the wages earned by their male co-workers.[12]

Clerical and Sales Jobs

In 1973 more than 11 million workers were employed in clerical jobs—a figure that has no doubt increased since that time—while 2.2 million were in sales jobs. Office work was originally a male job, but with the introduction of the typewriter women moved into jobs as typists and clerks with astonishing speed and in great numbers. In fact, the occupational group increased by 68 percent in the period 1968 to 1973 alone, in part because of the increase in office temporaries. Thirty-four percent of American women workers are employed in clerical work and 7 percent in saleswork, making this group account for more than 40 percent of all American women who work for pay.

Saleswork has the largest pay gap between men's and women's median earnings, a reflection in part of the specializations that women were encouraged (or permitted) to enter. About two-thirds of all the women in this category are retail salesclerks. Women have seldom been hired, in the past, as sales representatives for big companies. Bird notes the curious inside/outside dichotomy in job assignment: women were permitted to represent the company as receptionists in the home office but not as salesworkers on their own away from the home site.[13]

Since the last census, women have made significant inroads into the male-dominated occupations of real estate broker and insurance agent, although in the latter category, according to one source, they earn less overall than the men. An interesting occupational analysis of travel agencies

[12] *1975 Handbook on Women Workers* (Washington, D.C.: U.S. Department of Labor, 1975), pp. 105, 135, 287.
[13] Caroline Bird, with Sara Welles Briller, *Born Female: The High Cost of Keeping Women Down* (New York: Pocket Books, 1971 rev. ed.).

showed that men were predominant in the management posts and women in sales.[14]

Clerical workers? This group includes 3 million secretaries, 1.1 million stenographers, 1.5 million bookkeepers, nearly a million cashiers, and thousands of bank tellers, receptionists, counter clerks, file clerks, statistical clerks, telephone operators, and teachers' aides. A recent study of this occupation concluded that the introduction of "word processing" and the increased specialization of tasks have led to a "proletarianization" of clerical work, a development that may well impair the efficiency the changes aimed to promote.[15]

Tepperman has identified a number of myths about office work that clerical workers themselves often believe. Among them: that there are many opportunities for advancement into management; that the clerical job is a secure and protected one, being so close to management that it is virtually part of it; and that the clerical workers' contributions to the company effort are respected and rewarded by a salary commensurate with the responsibilities undertaken. Each of these is false, Tepperman believes, citing as evidence the small number of middle managers who started as clericals, the high incidence of lay-offs of clericals in times of recession, and the low salaries that pervade the occupation.[16] Kanter cites the example of "secretaries who do work that is so low skill and replaceable that their only way to get recognition and perhaps advancement is to develop a relationship of personal service with a boss, only to find themselves tied further to that boss and rewarded for things that are not generalizable or useful anywhere else in the organization." [17]

[14] Lewis A. Mennerick, "Organizational Structuring of Sex Roles in a Nonstereotyped Industry," *Administrative Science Quarterly,* Vol. 20 (December 1975), pp. 570–586.

[15] Evelyn Nakana Glenn and Roslyn L. Feldberg, "Degraded and Deskilled: The Proletarianization of Clerical Work," *Social Problems,* Vol. 25 (October 1977), pp. 52–64.

[16] Jean Tepperman, *Not Servants, Not Machines: Office Workers Speak Out* (Boston: Beacon Press, 1976), pp. 197–235.

[17] Kanter, p. 11.

Sixteen percent of American women workers who are college graduates are employed as clericals, as are 6 percent of those who have undertaken a year or more of graduate study.[18] Sometimes (although not always or exclusively) these well-educated clericals are the ones who land the coveted jobs as private secretaries. Sometimes these jobs are mixed blessings. In many companies a secretary's future is tied to that of her boss. As he advances, she may (although not automatically) follow. Clerical workers lack autonomy and decision-making power on the job; the jobs are often a bitter disappointment to college women, in part because their training in the liberal arts has not prepared them for the work they are expected to undertake.

The Professions and Management

Greenwood has described a profession as an occupation characterized by (1) a need for specialized training; (2) a body of theory; (3) shared norms, rules, and patterns of socializing; and (4) a shared code of ethics and an acceptance on the part of the community of the professional's claim to expertise.[19] There is a long-standing debate about personnel work: Is it merely a trade or an exalted profession? To sidestep that controversy here, we will define a profession as an occupation that calls for credentialing at the graduate level.

Using this yardstick, we can count many occupations both in the private sector and in public service as professional. About 15 percent of women workers are in the professions; approximately the same proportion of men workers are. But there the similarity ends. Men are distributed in a broad range of professions, while women are concentrated in four:

[18] *1975 Handbook on Women Workers*, p. 189.
[19] Ernest Greenwood, "Attributes of a Profession," *Social Work*, Vol. 2 (July 1957), pp. 45–55.

1. Teaching (except college teaching)
2. Social work
3. Library work
4. Nursing

These four occupations, while dignified, and important, are also sometimes termed "semiprofessions." [20] What else do these four professions have in common?

1. Each commands comparatively low pay for the high education required.
2. Each is a predominantly female occupation with predominantly male leadership.[21]
3. Each has a comparatively unfavorable projection of job openings in the 1980s. The number of applicants will exceed the number of openings for teachers at all levels, it appears. Social workers, librarians, and nurses will find increasing specialization and credentialing required for qualification.

Perhaps more compelling is the observation that these four professions can be seen as extensions of the role that women perform at home as mothers and homemakers. Mothers teach, counsel, care for the sick, and serve as guardians of common culture, which they pass on to the next generation. These honorable activities are not well rewarded in the world of work.

About 5 percent of all women workers are employed as managers: a total of over 1.5 million. Like women professionals, women managers hold different types of jobs from their male counterparts. While a male manager is likely to

[20] Richard L. Simpson and Ida H. Simpson, "Women and Bureaucracy in the Semi-Professions," in Amitai Etzioni (ed.), *The Semi-Professions and Their Organization: Teachers, Nurses, Social Workers* (New York: Free Press, 1969).

[21] James W. Grimm and Robert N. Stern, "Sex Roles and Internal Labor Market Structures: The 'Female' Semi-Professions," *Social Problems*, Vol. 21, No. 5, June 1974, pp. 690–705.

be in the corporate world ("Manager, Western Advertising Division, XYZ Company"), a woman is more likely to be managing a food store, an apparel store, or a restaurant. In the corporate world she is sometimes found as an office manager (a supervisor of secretaries) or as a manager of a training section, a benefits division, a housekeeping division, or a records and editing section. The very functions of teacher, nurse, social worker, and librarian that women serve in the professions are echoed in the managerial jobs they hold.

The lack of women leaders in the corporate world has been explained in terms that are somewhat unflattering to women as a group. These explanations can be grouped into three types:

1. Women don't dress for success or have the personality traits that have proved to be important factors linked with success for males.
2. Women are "queen bees" in that once they climb up the managerial ladder, they pull it up behind them rather than helping younger women. Once in the executive suite, women slam the door.[22]
3. Women may say that they want to be leaders, but secretly they have a "fear of success" that impedes their achievement.

The first of these explanations (debunked in part in Chapter 5) seems to rely heavily on support from advertisers and fashion designers who make a living by persuading women that new clothes are better than old clothes. The "queen bee" explanation, favored by some male psychologists, has little support from data. Terborg has found no evidence that women are less supportive of apprentices than men are.[23] In fact, Edith Lynch finds that

[22] Graham Staines et al., "The Queen B. Syndrome," *Psychology Today*, Vol. 7, No. 8 (January 1974), p. 55.
[23] James R. Terborg, "Women in Management: A Research Review," *Journal of Applied Psychology*, Vol. 62, No. 6 (December 1977), p. 656.

women at the top are lonesome and eager to help younger women along.[24]

The "fear of success" explanation—based on Matina Horner's findings that women tend to see success and femininity as mutually exclusive—is harder to counter. The explanation may have merit, although there have been problems in replicating Horner's studies.[25]

In 1969 Horner tested college students by asking them to complete a sentence. Two different versions were used. When the sentence read "At midterms, John found himself at the head of his medical school class . . . ," students tended to predict a happy and successful career for John. When the sentence read "At midterms, *Joan* found herself at the head of her medical school class . . . ," students were less sanguine about her future. Some women reported that she did nothing but study and thus had an unhappy social life; others refused to accept the premise and wrote that there had been a mistake: it turned out, they said, that Joan's boyfriend was at the head of the class and she was second. Clearly, success for women was viewed as riskier than it was for men.

Perhaps one problem in replicating these studies in other settings is that the experiment is now familiar. Many subjects are sophisticated. Respondents who know that the researcher is prompted by an interest in the male/female dimension may well respond differently from those who are (as they say) naive subjects.

An example of such sophistication at an early age came about on a college campus. A four-year-old girl went with her mother on a Saturday to visit the college nursery school. Looking around the playroom, the little girl called to her mother, "Look! Here's one of those funny mirrors on the wall." Her mother was astounded that she knew about such things. It was clear that she did, for the child went on to

[24] Edith M. Lynch, *The Executive Suite: Feminine Style* (New York: AMACOM, 1973), passim.

[25] Matina Horner, "Fail: Bright Women," *Psychology Today*, Vol. 3, No. 6 (November 1969), pp. 36–38, 62.

explain that that mirror was a special kind—"people on the other side can see in here."

Sometimes the neatest experiments are the ones that cannot be repeated. One Australian psychologist saw a golden chance to test a hypothesis when he was introducing an American guest lecturer to each of his six classes. To the first class, he introduced the visitor as a professor; to the second, as an associate professor; to the third, as an assistant professor; to the fourth as a lecturer; to the fifth, as a teaching assistant; and to the last class, as a visiting student. After each class he queried the students about the visitor, asking them among other things how tall the speaker was. The estimates dwindled as the day progressed. There was a clear link between the students' perceptions of the speaker's height and the status they thought he had.

An interesting extension of the "fear of success" hypothesis was undertaken by Lois Hoffman, who went back to the original subjects tested by Horner a decade earlier. Her interest: to see if the careers of the women who showed fear of success when they were students varied from the careers of those women who displayed little "FOS." Her preliminary analysis of the case histories suggested an interesting hypothesis. Women who are high on FOS may try, she says, to maintain a balance between the status of their husbands (or boyfriends) and their own. Perhaps they are seeking men who are a little bit smarter, more successful, and richer than they are. When that balance shifts, when the woman herself shows signs of achieving more than her husband, the woman tries perhaps unknowingly to restore the original balance. Hoffman cites the cases of women who quit work when they were promoted and their husbands weren't. When a husband lost his job, the working wife would restore the balance by another mechanism, one that seemed irrational in terms of their financial situation at the time: she'd get pregnant.[26]

---

[26] Lois Hoffman, presentation made at Cornell University, New York State College of Human Ecology, Ithaca, N.Y., April 28, 1977.

It is clear that the explanations for all human behavior are complicated and hard to tease out. What we can say, however, from the evidence presented in this chapter, is that the work women do for pay is quite different from the work men do. Among blue collar workers, women in the skilled trades (where the money and prestige are) constitute a statistically insignificant number. Saleswomen are selling clothes (and, more recently, larger commission items like insurance) mainly to women; clerical workers are drowning in the typing pool, and many see placement as a private secretary for one boss as a lifeline. Women classified as managers often manage enterprises that are related to the "women's professions" of nursing, teaching, library work, and social work.

Women have seldom ventured into predominantly male occupations in the past. This pattern may change considerably in the future. Still, an April 1977 Gallup poll showed that girls and boys continue to report considerably different career aspirations. Following are the top ten career choices for each group, in order of preference:

Girls	*Boys*
1. Secretary	1. Skilled worker
2. Teacher	2. Engineer
3. Nurse	3. Lawyer
4. Other medical	4. Teacher
5. Veterinarian	5. Professional athlete
6. Fashion design/modeling	6. Musician
7. Doctor	7. Architect
8. Social worker	8. Farmer
9. Business	9. Doctor
10. Cosmetologist/hairdresser	10. Military

The personnel practitioner who seeks to provide truly equal opportunity for both sexes will recognize that although most workers appear to be following traditional lines for their sex, there are exceptions. The new legislation is designed to protect not only the exceptions but the other women and girls who may not yet realize that the brains and talent are equally divided between the male and female skulls. Male jobs are male only by custom. Custom dies hard, but nothing will speed its demise faster than the laws that protect both women and men from outdated and mistaken ideas about the nature of women and men.

How long will it take? Hard to tell. A college student asked that question of William Shatner, the actor who played Captain Kirk in the TV series *Startrek*. Shatner gave a series of dramatic readings on a college campus in the fall of 1977. The student raised one question about the series. She noted that the writers seemed to be so imaginative about new life forms and new problems on other planets. How was it that there was no difference in the traditional relationship between the sexes on the spaceship *Enterprise*? The men were the leaders; the women, the helpers. "Ah," said Shatner, assuming his Captain Kirk demeanor and voice, "I believe women have the ability to be captains of spaceships. They've been discriminated against long enough. They can be leaders." There was silence from the 2,000 students present until he added a qualification that drew a roar of appreciative laughter. "Just not on my spaceship," he said. "Not on the *Enterprise*."

I used to like it when men opened the door for me. But now it irks me quite a bit, even when I tell myself they are only showing good manners. I can't help thinking that I have to pay a lot for that gallant custom. All that deference to us—and we still earn 58 cents for every dollar they do. I'd rather we'd have a really equal chance at work and really equal pay. Then if he's carrying something heavy, I'll open the door for him and he can do the same for me when I need help. But only then.

—*Comment overheard at a women's conference, 1974*

9

Day-to-Day Problems with and for Women Workers

IN 1889 the territory of Wyoming applied for admission to the union as a state. Women had been voting there and serving on juries since 1870. This posed a problem in Washington: How could Congress permit Wyoming to enter the union? As Susan B. Anthony and other women watched from the gallery, the legislators debated the constitutionality of women voting, the problems that would arise if the new state were to elect a woman to their group, and the "insoluble problem" of what such an elected congressman who was a woman would be called.[1] In the end, Wyoming was admitted. It was 31 years, however, before all women were granted the right to vote. And the seemingly trivial issue of what to call women who step out of traditional roles is still with us.

In this chapter we will consider such day-to-day problems as forms of address for women—not such a small matter to the personnel officer who has to put up with the furor that missteps cause. Next we will consider etiquette problems that have arisen as men and women work together as equals—and one imaginative solution to them—along with the delicate matter of some women's work habits and a possible way to help the woman who may lose perspective on the importance of her contribution to the total company effort. Finally, we will consider two problems that call for more complicated solutions. The first is the issue of bringing about attitude change. This is dismissed as unimportant by some feminists, but it has to be seen as a major issue when morale sags because of alleged "reverse discrimination." The second is the challenge of providing career ladders for all employees, men and women, white and black. Steps forward in this direction are the most important actions a corporation can take in bringing about equality between women and men of all races at work.

What Do Women Want—to Be Called?

A symbol of the changed view some women have about themselves can be seen in their heightened sensitivity about names and name styles. Forms of address can cause great trials in the personnel office, where the effort is just to

---

[1] Eleanor Flexner, *Century of Struggle: The Woman's Rights Movement in the United States* (New York: Atheneum, 1974), p. 178.

get the messages out to staff members and to sort their responses into appropriate folders. Routine communications elicit a flood of outrage because they are addressed in a way that offends somebody—the divorcée who no longer uses her husband's name, the young feminist who sees a sinister conspiracy in the fact that "those people in personnel keep calling me Miss instead of Ms," or the older woman who takes pride in being Mrs. and feels diminished when addressed as Ms by people she thought knew her by now.

Several years ago the American Association of University Women polled its members to determine if the married ones preferred to be addressed as Mrs. Mary Jones or Mrs. Robert Jones. The answers were divided about evenly, which suggested to the officers that they were in a no-win situation. However they set up the address labels, half their members would be offended. The most poignant complaint came from a personnel director who reported that one of his staff members "blithely changed her name five times in one year."

The best solution to this problem is, it appears, to honor all requests with patience and civility. It must be remembered that names are important to people. Communications coming from management should be addressed with attention to spelling and precise use of job titles. Name changes are not undertaken lightly, although it may seem so. There is judicial laughter when an "Ellen Cooperman" petitions to change her name to "Ellen Cooperperson." Before the personnel practitioner snickers, he or she should imagine the reactions of Malcolm X and Muhammed Ali if somebody had dared to deny them permission to take new names to express new images. Today, in all but a few states of the union, the young woman who marries may legally retain the name she was given at birth. It is only by custom that brides changed their names for so long. That heavy hand of custom seems oppressive to some women. The courts have ruled, in fact, that people can use any name they wish, providing there is no intent to defraud.

It is admittedly a nuisance to differentiate women staff

members in three ways: the "Misses," the "Mrs.'s," and the "Ms's." (This is, of course, why feminists advanced the title of Ms in the first place—because they wished an undifferentiated title like Mr. that would keep their marital status their own business. The fact that the use of Ms is still a political statement in 1978 suggests that they did not succeed.) If changing a name is annoying for those who keep personnel records, it is ten times more of a production for the name changer herself. And she knows it and still does it, so personnel should respond in kind.

The compiler of a staff directory at one work organization was so inundated with outraged calls that she had to discontinue the tradition of including information about marital status by each name. By custom, the names of married people had been marked with asterisks. It was a handy system when employers and their spouses were invited to social functions. Secretaries bungled less when they used the directory rather than trying to remember if "Paul Jones in purchasing is married or not." A complication, however, was that some staff members listed in the directory as unmarried were in fact halves of couples who lived together (as they say) without benefit of clergy. In any case, the custom is gone. Management decided to refrain from making information about marital status public.

Practitioners need to be cautious with language. A woman who has been in domestic service where she was forever addressed by her first name takes pride in hearing herself called Mrs. or Miss, as the case may be. In contrast, a person in the research department with a hard-won Ph.D. finds it offensive to be addressed as Mrs. Jones when her male colleagues are saluted with Dr. A recent study of name styles suggests that nonexempt women may indeed take pleasure in being called Mrs., especially at job levels where other sources of satisfaction are limited.[2] Courtesy suggests that we all call people what they ask to be called. Use Ms if they prefer; forget it if they don't. Common

---

[2] Jennie Farley, "Women at Work: Name Styles and Job Level," *Journal of Employment Counseling,* Vol. 13, No. 4 (December 1976), pp. 174–181.

sense suggests avoiding any jests at the expense of women (including the themes of nagging mothers-in-law, dumb blondes, dopey women drivers, little old ladies in tennis shoes, and Jewish mothers). Shakespeare was correct when he wrote, "He jests at scars who never felt a wound."

A final caveat. The communicator in personnel should scrutinize all memorandums carefully to make certain they do not transmit information that is inappropriate for some readers. One example is the formal invitation sent to each member of the engineering staff inviting "you and your wife" to a social function. Not well received by the two women engineers with no wives to bring. One of the three women in the United States who serve as chief of police still remembers that the letter inviting her to take the oral examination after the preliminary screening was addressed to "Mr. Kay Good." [3] And women attending conferences mainly attended by males wish they would not be sent name tags marked "Stick this in your shirt pocket."

Old Social Customs in the New Work Situation

Traditional rules still govern much of the interaction between the sexes. Some people have noted, in fact, that it is easier to change the law than it is to change the habits of language and behavior that we learn as children. An Ohio State sociologist who studied rules of etiquette extensively found that male students reported "feeling angry and castrated when a woman 'purposefully beats a man to the door and opens it,' while women students reported feeling unfeminine and unprotected when they do not receive such courtesies." [4] Although such extreme reactions seem hard to believe, it may be that, as sociologist Goffman says, "the

[3] Terry Wetherby, "Up Close with Women Who Hold 'Men's Jobs,'" *New Woman,* January–February 1978, p. 46. Reprinted from Terry Wetherby, *Conversations—Working Women Talk About Doing a Man's Job* (Milbrae, Cal.: Les Femmes, 1977).

[4] Laurel Richardson Walum, *The Dynamics of Sex and Gender: A Sociological Perspective* (Chicago: Rand McNally, 1977), pp. 7–8.

gestures which we sometimes call empty are perhaps the fullest things of all." [5]

Men are supposed to open doors for women, light their cigarettes, help them with their coats, walk next to them on the street side when outdoors, and participate in a whole array of rituals that are inconvenient at work. Most people modify their habits to suit new situations without much difficulty. In fact, one "female corporate jock" reported a salutary effect of being the first woman to reach her level in management. Each time she reached for a cigarette, the men made such a production of lighting it for her, with gallant flourishes and intimate hand touches, that she said to herself the equivalent of "forget this." She quit smoking. [6]

Others find that old habits bring about less desirable changes in the work situation. A personnel practitioner in a steel company reports that one of the least-sought-after jobs in the mill operation is "trucker's assistant"—a general helper to the driver of one of the biggest rigs on the road. When something goes wrong, the assistant is supposed to jump out, run around to the back, and make the adjustments as fast as possible—in short, to do everything to make life easier for the truck driver. Now, under a consent decree, women can bid for that job; they do. One trucker's assistant and the driver she assists find themselves acting out a foolish ritual when they hear something flapping on their load. He jumps down, runs around, opens the door for her; she gets down, goes to the back, fixes what's wrong, climbs back in. They carry on until something else needs checking. Then he hops out again, runs around, opens the door for her. . . .

A related problem arose in another organization among the custodians. Until recently, the women were classified as maids and earned less money than the male custodians did.

[5] Erving Goffman, *Interaction Ritual* (Garden City, N.Y.: Doubleday/Anchor, 1967), p. 91; cited in Walum, p. 25.

[6] Donald O. Jewell, "The Female Corporate Jock: What Price Equality?" *Atlanta Economic Review*, Vol. 26, No. 2 (March–April 1976),pp. 25–31.

The only difference in their work was that the men did high windows from the inside and carried out the trash. The two job classifications were merged, and both the former maids and the men were classified as custodians, at the same rate of pay. The merger represented a considerable increase for the women. And they appreciated the fact that the men gallantly continued to do the high windows and take out the garbage.

A third example comes from a factory where the personnel people noticed that many women were asking to be transferred to the dirtiest department where the heaviest weights had to be lifted. Curious as to why this should be, they visited the department and observed the workers. Then they understood. The men were doing the heavy lifting for the women.

The decision in the personnel office in each of these cases was to do nothing. The feeling was that workers often organize a division of labor. So long as nobody complains, fine. If two women reached such a mutually acceptable agreement, nobody would intervene. If two men did, there'd be no interference. So let the woman and the man work it out.

One who would take issue with this decision is Nancy Kaye Andersen, a butcher:

> When I went to work in this shop, the manager said that he looked at me as a woman meatcutter and he didn't expect me to lift as much as the other guys. He said, "If I ever tell you to go into the cooler to get something and it's too heavy, have one of the guys help you. I don't object." He said that *he* asks for help a lot of times, too.
>
> But I think that there's no reason that a woman should be a burden to males working in the same shop. If she can't pull the weight, I think she should get out.[7]

Addressing this same problem in the office, Richard Saltzmann advises supervisors to avoid shortchanging

[7] Quoted in Wetherby, p. 45.

women by helping them too much. He recounts the case of
the manager who corrected his woman assistant's work
himself before passing it on. If the men assistants erred, the
manager sent their reports back for revision. Saltzmann
concludes: "On the surface, Miss Kirchner is getting away
with murder; in fact, she's being denied the chance to learn,
to grow on the job, to perform up to her abilities." [8]

If a gallant response to the presence of women at the
work site appears to cause difficulties, the opposite reaction
can cause even more. At AT&T there were "gibes and ostra-
cism inflicted on women who had gravitated into formerly
all-male jobs. A woman engineer, the only one in her department, ate lunch alone for a year and a half. Her meal-
time isolation ended only when another woman engineer
joined the department." [9] According to an article in *Worklife*, women's reactions to hazing differ. A union painter at a
submarine yard in Groton, Connecticut, reported that "usually the younger men offer to help . . . with the heavy
buckets of paint, while the older men complain about the
distraction." She takes catcalls from the male workers as "a
kind of compliment."

Rich reports that an automotive machinist's apprentice
in Seattle was "discouraged by obscene photographs she'd
find taped up in the cab of a truck she was working on. But
when she discovered, in the nuts and bolts bin, a large, ugly
doll with sexual parts added by a crudely imaginative local
craftsman, she'd had it. . . . She resigned." More extreme
was the incident reported by a female carpenter's apprentice in Bakersfield, California. By her account, two jour-
neymen cornered her, ordered her to quit, and, when she
refused, smashed her thumbs with a hammer. As Rich
notes, this kind of violence could be banished and even
mild harassment diminished "if contractors were obliged to

---

[8] Richard R. Saltzmann, "Working with Women: How & Where & Why
& When—Plus Five Ways to Bumble," *Marketing Times,* Vol. 24, No. 2
(March–April 1977), pp. 12–15.

[9] Georgette Jasen, "Ma Bell's Daughters," *The Wall Street Journal,*
February 28, 1978, p. 1.

abide by the proposed regulations issued last fall." The proposed regulations set a higher goal for the percentage of women in construction jobs and oblige contractors to maintain a working environment free of harassment, intimidation, and coercion.[10]

One woman trucker in Emeryville, California, attributes her work problems to management. Her suit alleges that her road test was far more grueling than that given to the men and that "company brass vandalized two of her cars, boobytrapped her equipment, and fired her twice for no good reason." Her complaint is against company officials, not male truckdrivers, who, she said, "have treated me just like a lady." [11]

Most of the problems don't involve smashed thumbs or lawsuits, just a little adjustment here and there. An attorney recalls that a judge she held in high esteem stopped her on the way to a meeting. He had a problem, he said. He was going to tell a "naughty story" and she would be the only woman in the big group of members of the bar present. Then he brightened up. "I'll whistle when I get to that word," he said. And made his stately way into the courtroom.

She went in with the men, feeling somewhat conspicuous as the only woman. But she was truly embarrassed when, as he was telling his story, he interrupted himself to explain to all in that huge meeting that since there was a lady present, he'd whistle at the bad word. And he did.

A manager of equal opportunity agency relations at General Electric echoes that sentiment:

> Although women are certainly headed in the right direction, we still encounter occasional annoyances to which men are not subjected. For instance, I cringe every time a man swears, or tells an off-color joke, and then feels the

[10] Les Rich, "Hardhatted Women in Construction," *Worklife*, February 1978, pp. 1, 15.
[11] "Woman Trucker Files Suit," *Ithaca (N.Y.) Journal*, March 10, 1978, p. 17.

need to apologize for it. I'll never forget one particular meeting when I was the only woman in attendance. Someone told a risqué story, after which the chairperson immediately rose to point out that we were in mixed company. That action alone singled me out. But he further compounded the problem with an unnecessary apology. Actually, I thought the joke was rather funny, and have since told it to a number of people. . . . And certainly no apologies were necessary. I think most women feel like I do—we'd prefer not to be singled out with unnecessary special attention.[12]

A management consultant reports that successful women often have that irritating experience in business meetings:

Every time the word "damn" or "hell" escapes a man's lips in a business setting, he immediately turns to apologize abjectly to any woman present. Since these mildly emphatic expletives can punctuate every other sentence when men get into heated discussions, the "pardon me" apologia to women becomes unbearably repetitive. One woman executive told me that a male colleague interrupted himself fourteen times in ten minutes and finally turned to her in anger and said, "Dammit, you'll just have to get used to this talk if you think you're going to be in business!"

She hadn't said a word! Her question to me was, "Is it possible that any reasonably intelligent man in the mid-1970s really *believes* that a woman never heard the word 'damn' or 'hell' in her life?" [13]

Luckily, this is a question that personnel practitioners do not as a rule have to deal with. As men get tired of apologizing or swearing (or both), that issue will disappear. It will be interesting to see what takes its place. Many a bright

---

[12] "When the Boss Is a Woman," *For Your Information* (Public Affairs Section, General Electric), Vol. 1, No. 4 (December 1977), p. 2.
[13] Betty Lehan Harragan, *Games Mother Never Taught You* (New York: Rawson Associates, 1977), pp. 82–83.

young man has made his way up the corporate ladder because of his ability to have the right jokes for the right occasion—just the thing to put people at ease. And now the jokes may be censored by the teller himself.

Not all the problems are in men's heads of course. Newly promoted women often have difficulty putting their own work in persepctive. Management consultant Betty Harragan notes that almost every employee puffs up the importance of his or her own job when writing job descriptions. The puffing can extend to the workplace as well. Harragan cites the case of an advertising copy chief in a department store who worked nights, Saturdays, and Sundays turning out advertisements that were "polished gems of perfect English, quixotic humor, and clever artwork." When it was pointed out to the copy chief that she was not seeing her job in proper perspective and might be overemphasizing secondary considerations, she saw the point.

> For twenty years, I thought my job was to turn out the best advertising copy I could possibly conceive for the store. It never occurred to me that my sole task was to attract enough customers to move the advertised merchandise. . . . I treated every ad for 89¢ panties as if we were writing "Ode to a Nightingale." [14]

Harragan advises women to try to survey their own jobs from a managerial perspective. The personnel manager who finds women or men employees with this problem might counsel them to think along these lines. But not everyone changes attitudes as readily as the ad chief.

Attitude Change

While many employees may declare themselves to be in favor of equal pay for equal work, comparatively few truly consider women's work to be of equal value to men's. The

[14] Harragan, pp. 120–121.

manager who regularly takes extra time at noon to play handball without a flicker of conscience, knowing he puts in plenty of extra hours at night, may resist the institution of flextime for clerical workers because it would not be businesslike. As secretaries know full well, many executives who complain of their heavy workload and of their lack of efficient help still walk from their desks to the outer office to ask somebody else to dial a telephone number. They fume at the introduction of authorization numbers and WATS lines and extra complications in direct-dialing procedures and seem unable to keep their own papers in order and appointments in mind. They resent the time their secretaries take for coffee, not recognizing that those breaks are, it appears, richly deserved.

A study undertaken in 1977 by the Survey Research Center of the activities of 376 working men and women suggests that while the average man spends 52 minutes of each working day not working, the average woman spends only 35. "Not only do women work more," the researchers report, "they work harder. A 'work effort scale,' based on individuals' reports of the level of energy they expend while at work, reveals that the effort given to the job by women is 112 percent of that given by men." [15]

Men can sometimes make women uncomfortable by commenting on their appearance. A woman engineer reports that her co-workers fell into that habit. She tried to ignore it but found herself becoming increasingly irritated. If she wore trousers, the men would say, "Too bad, no skirt on Karen today." If she wore a dress, they'd comment at length (with perhaps the kindest of intentions), asking one another, "Did you catch Karen?" Finally, she got tired of that subject and wore a kind of uniform: trousers, white shirt, jacket. "When I looked more like them," she recounted later, "they didn't bring it up all the time. They are nice guys but they didn't seem to hear me when I'd ask them to give it a rest."

It should be noted that some women, especially those

[15] *ISR Newsletter* (Institute for Social Research, Ann Arbor, Michigan), October 1977, p. 8.

moving into a new job, feel uncertain about what constitutes proper clothing. Their counterparts, male newcomers, have only to look around to have their questions answered. But women sometimes waver between buying the "dress for success" theme so prominent in management books and fashion magazines and feeling guilty that they are putting too much emphasis on the exterior package.

A seemingly trivial issue that surfaces every year on college campuses is symbolic of the unease some young women feel. They ask anxiously if they have to wear dresses to be interviewed. Some even feel that it would be dishonest to masquerade as conformists when they are (or fancy themselves to be) free spirits. That proves to be, in fact, the easiest question to answer. One career counselor responds to the query with admirable brevity: "Nobody ever lost out on a job because she dressed too conservatively."

Men need to be, it seems, understanding about women who in their eagerness to please seem to mouth socially acceptable statements without thinking through what is truly meant. Showing copies of a superb transcript of grades, they may anxiously assure the interviewer that their families come first. Indeed, there is something about the social image of women that seems to make that statement mandatory. Successful actresses, people who have clearly devoted themselves single-mindedly to a career, seem obliged to remark in interviews that their real fulfillment lies in cooking and sewing.

We expect a man to say his family comes first. Let us hope it does. Men are seldom asked. But women are asked, and the nature of the question appears to require the answer it virtually always elicits. Perhaps an extreme example is the interview with a woman rabbinical student. Clearly, she had been accepted because of her skills and merit as a future rabbi. But she reports in a newspaper column that her greatest joy comes from helping her fellow students who are male. She makes them soup and does their laundry and mending.

For women to feel comfortable in unfamiliar settings (as

for men in similar circumstances), they have to be treated just like their peers. This attitude cannot be legislated by top management or by personnel. But both should remember the results of a study undertaken in 1969 at Cornell. Students in introductory social science courses were divided at random into discussion sections at the beginning of the term. On Mondays and Wednesdays, all the students heard the same lecture at the same hour in the same lecture room. On Fridays, they met separately in small groups for discussion sections, with each section guided by a different graduate student. At the end of the term, it was clear that what went on in discussion section was important. The students' evaluations of the lecture they heard on Monday and Wednesday varied markedly according to which discussion section they attended on Fridays. This suggests strongly that professors had better recognize graduate discussion leaders for what they are: influential members of the teaching team. All the careful preparation of lectures could go for naught because of something that went on in discussion section.

Just as a teaching assistant can torpedo a professor's course, so a line manager can destroy top management's affirmative action program. The manager's attitudes can lead workers to evaluate the overall effort quite differently than if they had been in another department. If a company wants to get full benefit from its affirmative action policies, it is well advised to get the line managers' cooperation. One way is transmit that simple fact: supervisors are important, and management recognizes it; they will be rewarded for full and sincere efforts and not for lip service.

It is clear that professors cannot police every graduate student's interaction with every undergraduate, nor can top managers monitor every social exchange between supervisors and newly hired or promoted women or minority men. But the importance of what goes on at the one-to-one level becomes clear when those interactions produce such bitterness that the professoriate or top management is discredited—and held liable.

Building Career Ladders

Maryluise Satterfield, drawing on 20 years of experience in the New York State Department of Civil Service, asserts that there are no sharply defined career ladders for clerical workers either in her unit (the Department of Mental Hygiene) or apparently elsewhere in state service. One problem, she notes, is a misunderstanding about what really constitutes a career ladder. It is not more pay for work currently being done, for seniority, or for merit; it is not job enrichment (as meritorious as that may be) or job rotation. Nor is it a series of jobs unrelated to each other. The ideal career ladder, as Satterfield defines it, is an arrangement of related jobs in successive levels of difficulty and responsibility. Ideally, employees begin at the lowest levels and receive training and gain experiences that help (but do not mandate) their advancement.

A survey of 400 women clericals in the state service uncovered good news—and bad. The most heartening finding was that 38 percent of those surveyed had some college training after they were hired, and a full 64 percent had taken courses aimed toward job advancement. So there was keen interest on the part of a majority to move into more challenging work. The discouraging finding, from the researchers' point of view, was that respondents appeared to have little idea how that move was to be made. In response to a question about how change could be brought about, 11 percent signified that they would wait and see, 85 percent gave answers suggesting that management should take some action, and only 4 percent signified that they intended to take further steps themselves. There seemed to be an air of passivity about the clerical workers, almost as though they were maidens in distress waiting patiently to be rescued.

Satterfield predicts, however, that some sort of career ladder for clerical workers will be created within the decade. She feels that it will be too short, probably ending in the job of administrative aide, with no access to higher rungs from that vantage point. (See Chapter 6 for research evidence on this point.) Clerical workers themselves will probably build in a requirement for too much training at each step, she notes; management should be alert to avoid that pitfall if it sincerely desires to utilize the talents of clerical workers to the fullest.[16]

Vogel and others see widespread unionization of clerical workers as inevitable and as a development management should be prepared to accept.[17] Most other observers, however, note that the long tradition of "unions are for blue collar people" will prevail. Even if large numbers of women clericals are moved to (or prevailed upon to) join existing unions, there will still be little massive change, since the development of opportunities for secretaries will not be a high priority with the majority of trade unionists, who are neither female nor stalled at the typewriter.

As noted earlier, all women workers are thought to be providing a second income to their families and, as such, to have limited commitment to the job. Statistics show, however, that fully 39 percent of the single women workers in 1973 were clericals and that the number of single parents among clerical workers is growing.[18] So there appears to be clear economic need, coupled with expressed desire for advancement, on the part of many clerks, secretaries, and typists.

Of course, the major question must be to what extent employers will find it in their self-interest to devote more resources to the issue. Reexamining and restructuring the clerical workforce will involve more radical changes than any other step proposed here, if only because of the numbers involved.

---

[16] Maryluise Satterfield, "Career Ladders for Clerical Workers," presentation made at Cornell University, New York State School of Industrial and Labor Relations, Ithaca, N.Y., October 5, 1977.

[17] Alfred Vogel, "Your Clerical Workers Are Ripe for Unionism," *Harvard Business Review*, Vol. 49, No. 2 (March–April 1971), pp. 48–54.

[18] *1975 Handbook on Women Workers* (Washington, D.C.: U.S. Department of Labor, 1975), p. 101.

Until such time as clerical work is modified and the nature of the opportunities broadened, what can individual managers do? Here, as elsewhere, dignity, autonomy, and security seem sadly lacking. The sensitive supervisor will strive to create an atmosphere where individual differences of workers can be respected and careful and conscientious work rewarded. The supervisor can take such simple steps as permitting or encouraging (or, if warranted, commanding) clerical workers to take responsibility for the work they themselves do. The secretary who undertakes research work should sign the report; she should be encouraged to initiate correspondence and sign it herself, not only in her supervisor's absence but as an independent worker; she should be invited to experiment with new procedures for handling the work flow and new methods of reporting. These seem to be small matters, but they make the difference between deadly routine and a diverse set of tasks that can be approached with imagination and enthusiasm.

In the early days of the women's movement, many clerical workers took umbrage at the arrogance and condescension they encountered among feminists. The speaker on a college campus who tells undergraduate women that 12 percent of the clerical workers in the civil service have bachelor's degrees frequently transmits to secretaries present that theirs is a fate worse than death. Freshly graduated college women, with their majors in medieval studies and Romance literature, drop into the personnel departments of large companies and allow as how they've "decided to take a little secretarial job" until opportunities in their own field open up. It comes as a sorry shock to them that they do not have the training or skills (or in some cases the tact) to hold a responsible job like secretary.

There is nothing inherently demeaning in secretarial work—indeed, it is honorable and important. Part of its bad image has come from the fact that college women with liberal arts training have not yet recognized the home truth that BA degrees (unlike bachelor of engineering degrees) are not designed to ready a recipient for work. Such undergraduate training must be supplemented with professional graduate work. Just as men go on to law school or business school with their bachelor of arts degrees, so women must obtain additional training to prepare themselves for the responsible jobs they want. It may be that the skills of college women are underutilized in clerical posts. It is clear that as most secretarial jobs are currently structured, they are. An examination of the nature of clerical work, with the aim of ascertaining how incumbents who show promise and inclination to advance can best be helped, may pay off in the long run for the corporate world. But this is a long-range aim, and the immediate gains may be comparatively few.

Companies, colleges, school systems, and state services outside big cities know the problem well. Personnel officers at a big university in a small town face the issue virtually hourly. The operation generates many words that somebody has to type. The opportunities for jobs are therefore largely (though not exclusively) confined to teaching and research posts on the one hand and clerical and service work on the other. The woman applicant without a Ph.D. is not qualified to teach or do research. Even though she brings experience as an editor or an elementary school teacher or a social worker or an administrator, or even has a master's degree, she is likely to find that her choice is between a clerical job or no job at all.

Is it the university's fault that it cannot provide a high-level professional job for every wife of every graduate student or junior faculty member? Hardly. But it does seem that the nature of the clerical jobs at each level should be reexamined so that talented people who respect the work can use their talents to further the interests of the organization. The challenge, as has been noted, is possibly the hardest one facing the concerned personnel practitioner, line manager, and top administrator.

Men can be overweight or alcoholic or
tee totalers or Don Juans and still be
accepted as "old Jim." But women
have to be just right—not too thin, not
too fat, not so prissy they won't take a
drink, and certainly not lushes, not
too young, not too old, certainly not
going on all the time about their children, not anything anybody can
criticize or they'll be *out*.

*—Advice from a panelist at a women's
conference on getting ahead in business.*

10

Worklife Problems
for Both Women
and Men

THE personnel practitioner can get heat from both the
feminist who seeks instant change in management policy
and the line manager who wants immediate waivers of legally mandated responsibilities. People in personnel can, of
course, grant neither. Enthusiasts on both sides periodi-
cally discover "new issues"—the very ones personnel has
been struggling with for years—and label them (depending

on their perspective) as gross inequities hitherto unnoticed
by anyone or as fresh examples of absurd demands that no
rational person outside of government would expect a manager to meet.

This chapter will consider five problems that personnel
is both thought to be ignorant of and expected to resolve the
moment they are mentioned. The problems are not new,
but they may well be exacerbated by the rising expectations
of government with respect to the power of law to eliminate
discrimination and of feminists with regard to the willingness of profitmaking companies to deal with the social problems faced by women. These issues, which are troublesome
both for women workers and for personnel managers, include the three "sex plus" problems—sex discrimination
based on age, sexual preference, and status as parent—the
prevention of sexual harassment on the job, and the "office
romance."

The "Sex Plus" Problems

Some women workers face problems over and above
their sex but related to it: they are parents, they are old, or
they are homosexual. Each brings a set of complications
that can make employers reluctant to have young mothers
or old women or lesbians in their companies. One can understand managers' reluctance, but one cannot agree that
any of these conditions alone is sufficient to deny an individual either employment in the first place or a fair chance
to work in peace once on the job.

The great increase in the female workforce in the last
decade has come about because, as noted earlier, mothers
of small children are much more likely to work for pay than
was the case in the past. Economist Juanita Kreps has demonstrated that women's pattern of labor force participation
is very different from that of men. When age is charted
against proportion working, the male pattern resembles an
arc: by and large, men enter the workforce and continue in

employment until they retire. Women's participation shows a sharp dip in the middle years—the childbearing lapse—then rises again as great numbers of women return to work when their children grow up. Students call this the M curve—M for mother.

This intermittent labor force participation is a uniquely American pattern. In no other country do so many women stay home when their children are little. But the pattern here is changing rapidly. The curve is approaching men's with every passing year, as fewer and fewer women either want to or can stay home with children. Grossman notes that nearly half the children in the United States now have mothers who work for pay.[1] There is every indication that that proportion will rise. One reason for the rise in the future may be that the daughter of a working mother is more likely to plan to work for pay than the daughter of a housewife.[2]

If mothers work, who—as Phyllis Schlafly asks over and over—*who* will take care of the children?[3] Perhaps the more pertinent question to ask is: Who *is* taking care of the children? About half the preschool children of working mothers are cared for in their own homes either by a relative or (much less frequently) by a hired caregiver. A third of the preschool children are taken to someone else's home, to be supervised by a relative or by a hired caregiver. Only 5 percent of preschool children are in group day care centers or nurseries. The others are taken to work by their mothers. As the children grow, the likelihood of their being cared for by a neighbor increases.

During World War II, when women's contribution to the workforce was sought, there were child care facilities in

[1] Allyson Sherman Grossman, "Almost Half of All Children Have Mothers in the Labor Force," *Monthly Labor Review,* Vol. 100, No. 6 (June 1977), pp. 41–48.

[2] Elizabeth M. Almquist, "Sex Stereotypes in Occupational Choice: The Case of College Women," *Journal of Vocational Behavior,* Vol. 5, No. 1 (August 1974), pp. 13–21.

[3] Phyllis Schlafly, quoted in Barbara Burke, "ERA Debate Like Cartoon Strip," *Ithaca (N.Y.) Journal,* January 26, 1978, p. 3.

abundance. After the war, when the women workers were let go to provide room for the returning veterans, the centers were closed. In the early 1970s there was a flurry of interest in company-sponsored child care centers; but today these centers, like the government-sponsored programs, are by and large gone or serving a limited population.

In the United States (unlike other modern countries), the care of small children is seen as a personal, not social, responsibility. Mothers who have to work are expected to make their own arrangements, and they do. Feminists have demanded that government and/or private industry take cognizance of the problem, but little has been done. One reason cited for the lack of federal and corporate response is that such social support for a working mother would *encourage* otherwise responsible mothers to leave their children. This attitude does not, unfortunately, take into account the harsh reality that many mothers of small children must work to eat.

George Milkovich's research suggests that it is to the company's advantage to provide onsite care, since this reduces both turnover and days lost by working mothers.[4] Other studies suggest that the provision of onsite care will serve the needs of some working mothers but by no means all. What appears needed is a network of facilities in the community to serve the diverse needs of residents. Parents who travel some distance to work prefer community facilities near their homes. Those with school-age children cannot take advantage of a company-provided center after school hours. A community center as envisioned by Harlow—one controlled by the parents, open at the hours when the parents work, willing to accept both infants and children of school age in the afternoons, providing for care of sick children, staffed in part by senior citizens, and available to all who need it—seems ideal.[5]

[4] George Milkovich, "A Few Overlooked Research Issues on the Way to Equal Opportunity," Working Paper 76-04, Industrial Relations Center, University of Minnesota, August 1976.
[5] Nora Harlow, *Sharing the Children: Village Child Rearing Within the City* (New York: Harper & Row/Colophon, 1975).

Until such centers come into being, companies can still help attack the problems faced by the working mother of small children. There are measures short of financing an entire child care center attached to the factory that may in fact be more effective, at least until (and if) the national conscience is aroused to the severity of the problem. A study undertaken in Tompkins County, New York, suggested that such stopgap measures may help very much indeed. Among the solutions proposed:

■ *The recognition that a woman's work performance may not reflect lack of commitment to the job.* If a hitherto responsible and reliable employee is absent more than usual over one winter, a casual look at her record may suggest that she just isn't as good as she used to be. The fact may be, however, that her child's illness is keeping her home. Once her child's ailment is cured, she is herself again. One personnel manager has devised a recordkeeping system for distinguishing between absences due to children's illness and those due to other causes. In this way he feels that his first-line supervisors will have more information about the individual worker's performance. One additional benefit, cited by the women workers who proposed the system, is that they no longer have to lie (masking their children's illnesses as their own) when they call in.

■ *The presence in personnel of a staff member who is knowledgeable about community child care resources and benefits.* Women report that, especially when they are new to a community, information about the availability of child care centers, drop-in centers, and people trained to take over when children are sick is difficult to come by. Such information is especially valuable to women who are already working and cannot seek help through service agencies during working hours. A small company could assign the responsibility to a person already on staff. Bigger organizations could hire or train a specialist to serve as liaison between the service agencies and the women who need them. The representative in turn could be part of a network of child care referral specialists in all companies in the community with working mothers.

■ *A system of granting parents a certain number of
leave days each year, to be taken when children are sick.*
These leave days could be taken by either father or mother.
Indeed, planners of all child care programs should recognize that the number of single parents is increasing and that
the increase is made up of working fathers as well as working mothers.

A second type of "sex plus" discrimination is that encountered by the older woman returning to the workforce.
As outlined earlier, she may suffer a collapse of confidence
as a result of her time out of the workforce. This helps her
not one whit in getting the equal consideration for a responsible job that she deserves. The experience of Catalyst,
Higher Education Resource Services (HERS), Washington
Opportunities for Women (WOW), and other groups seeking solutions to these problems has shown that the older
woman worker is a bargain for the company with imagination enough to hire her and promote her as warranted.

The presentation of credentials in the form of a businesslike résumé—seemingly a small matter—looms large in
the concerns of older women. A study of application forms
shows that even the most skilled and experienced returnees
tend to do themselves a disservice when they present their
credentials in writing.[6] A busy personnel officer turns away
from the amateurishly completed application because he or
she cannot imagine it represents an employable person.
The woman who answers the question "Type of job
sought?" with a phrase such as "Anything," "Any small way
I can help," or "My deepest interest has always been in
creativity" surely diminishes her chances of getting an
interview, never mind a job.

Sociologist Helena Lopata has noted that there are am-
biguities in the social definition of a housewife's role. She
outlines four stages through which the housewife passes:

[6] Jennie Farley, "Women Going Back to Work: Preliminary Problems,"
Journal of Employment Counseling, Vol. 7, No. 4 (December 1970), pp.
130–136.

1. Becoming—the new bride learns homemaking and learns to be a shopper and consumer of household goods.
2. Maintaining the expanding circle as she bears and rears small children.
3. Reaching the "full-house plateau."
4. Managing the shrinking circle as the children leave home.[7]

If we analyze this role progression as a career ladder, it can be seen that the ladder is in the form of a horseshoe. No matter how well the housewife does her job, it decreases relentlessly in importance as the children grow up. Indeed, some would say that the more effective she is in assisting her children to be independent, the sooner she will do herself out of a job.

As Lopata points out, the social role of housewife is a low-prestige job. It can gain in prestige, she notes, if the family members for whom the housewife provides staff support gain in prestige or increase in number. So it is that the wife of a famous man or mother of a famous child is honored. So it is that the housewife who has a great many children and perhaps aged parents depending on her may also be lauded.

In any case, she is, as a rule, retired in her prime. The wife of a corporate executive, as Kanter notes, is in unusual circumstances in that she is expected to provide helping services for her husband when he is starting out but has limited duties during his middle years. When and if he reaches top management, she is once again on call.[8] Women married to corporate presidents, college presidents, politicians, ministers, and high-level military men are among those whose jobs as wives are demanding at least intermit-

[7] Helena Znaniecki Lopata, "The Life Cycle of the Social Role of Housewife," in Marcello Truzzi (ed.), *Sociology in Everyday Life* (Englewood Cliffs, N.J.: Prentice-Hall, 1968), pp. 11–124.

[8] Rosabeth Moss Kanter, *Men and Women of the Corporation* (New York: Basic Books, 1977), pp. 105–115.

tently in the so-called golden years. But other wives are out of work at age 35, and it is they who need and deserve equal opportunity in the workplace. A representative of personnel can spot older women who need help by the fact that they often (and understandably) define themselves in terms of their husbands, using the "Mrs. John Jones" name style and including irrelevant information about their husbands' jobs or their children's activities in their applications for work.

It should be recognized that the older wife has every right to take credit for the success of members of her family. She may well have had a great deal to do with it. But this information is not pertinent to her job application. The casual discrimination against older women who have 25 years' potential working life ahead of them when they seek to reenter the workforce has not begun to be recognized. Banks are among the few institutions that truly welcome older women; their customs may spread to other organizations as more and more actions are instituted against violations of the law that protects both women and men from discrimination on the basis of age.

One sad footnote is that companies subject to consent degrees sometimes agree to favor some women over others. At least they are perceived to be acting that way. AT&T agreed to set up a management assessment program for women hired between 1965 and 1971 (to match one it had had for men hired during that period). Of those assessed, 43 percent were put on a "fast track" as "recommended women" but not without arousing resentment from women middle managers who had made it on their own. "Why shouldn't I be included?" complains a woman in middle management at New York Telephone Co. She started as a business office representative in 1951 and now says, "All I have is a law protecting old people." [9]

These two types of discrimination—on the basis of status as parent and of age—are intimately tied to sex discrimination. The link is apparent when we contrast the

[9] Georgette Jasen, "Ma Bell's Daughters," *The Wall Street Journal,* February 28, 1978, p. 1.

situation of women with that of men. There is clear legal precedent stating that a woman cannot be denied employment or promotion solely because she has small children unless a man with young children has the same restrictions placed on him.[10] Similarly, flight attendants have won the case based on the fact that stewardesses were considered "too old" to do the work when there were men of the same age in similar jobs. It is clear that women age socially before men do. President John F. Kennedy was 46 at the time of his assassination. His death was seen as especially poignant because he was cut down in his prime. A woman of 46 is not seen as so young. This assertion is difficult to prove—but it is clear, for example, that actors can be cast as romantic leads long after actresses their age are playing grandmothers.

A third type of "sex plus" discrimination has to do with homosexuality. The extent of employment discrimination based on sexual preference is little documented, but it seems clear that homosexuals who choose to identify themselves as such suffer problems in access to housing, opportunity to practice religion, freedom of speech, and freedom of assembly. One defense of current practices is that homosexuals are sick and, as is said, "queer." But the roots of homosexuality are nowhere clear, despite the assertion of some psychiatrists that the condition is pathological. Proponents of gay rights, as well as a substantial number of professional psychologists and psychiatrists, hold the condition to be normal though less common in the population than heterosexuality.

Early proponents of the idea that homosexuality was "within the normal range psychologically" were dismissed as biased or criticized for their methodology, since the majority of studies showed homosexuals to be less well adjusted than their opposite numbers who were heterosexual.[11] We can speculate that this maladjustment may be of

---

[10] Phillips v. Martin Marietta, 400 U.S. 542 (1971).

[11] Irving Bieber et al., *Homosexuality: A Psychoanalytic Study of Male Homosexuals* (New York: Vintage Books, 1962), pp. 17 ff.

social origin, a reaction to being discriminated against. However, if we accept the assumption that homosexuality is an illness, it may well be seen as a handicap entitling those who "suffer" from it to equal opportunities under the Rehabilitation Act.

Regardless of cause, homosexuality is a reality in American life and still carries with it a considerable social stigma, despite efforts of gay alliances. One personnel manager spoke for many when he said, "We have to think of the good of the whole community. If I were a banker and two men approached me for a loan to build a house, I'd certainly give it to the family man before I gave it to some gay." After reflection, he went on to say, "Why do they have to flaunt it? I guess I don't care what they do at home, but when they are so open about it I can't stomach it." And there, in a nutshell, is the best defense of gay rights. So long as homosexuals are denied credit, employment, advancement, loans, and housing, that long will they be fierce and furious about their sexual orientation. Should the day come when homosexuals are truly given equal treatment, when the old taboos are no more, they will no longer need to organize so militantly—a behavior that some find offensive whether it is undertaken by minority men or women of all races or homosexuals.

Lesbians carry an extra burden not borne by homosexual men. As females, they face limitations on their access to education, employment, and participation in political life. As lesbians, however, they know that they will have to support themselves; there will be no question of their working merely to "supplement their husbands' earnings."

This home truth was apparent to the lesbians at the National Women's Conference held in Houston, Texas, in November 1977. They worked hard to make certain that protection of their rights was among the resolutions included in the final roster. Indeed, it was. The resolution on sexual preference had three parts: first, that laws should be enacted to protect the civil rights of homosexuals; second, that state legislatures should repeal laws that restrict private sexual behavior between consenting adults; and third,

that child custody cases should be determined on the basis
of "which party is the better parent without regard to that
person's sexual and affectional orientation."

In November 1977 the Supreme Court refused to review
the case of James Gaylord, a homosexual high school
teacher in Tacoma, Washington, who was fired for "immor-
ality." [12] The issue was not his homosexual conduct, but his
status. The school board members asked Gaylord if he was
homosexual; he responded that he was. They dismissed
him. Now he says to fellow gays: "Lie if you are asked about
your sexual preference." Personnel managers may find that
any expression of views on the employment rights of
homosexuals will be scorned, because this is a class not yet
protected. But practitioners may find that their consciences
bother them if they do not stand up for gays.

Sexual Harassment at Work

The extent to which Title VII (or any other federal law)
protects women against harassment because they are
women is unclear. As Ginsburg and Koreski note, some judicial decisions suggest that sexual harassment is illegal;
other decisions are quite specific in considering that behavior beyond the purview of current law. In theory, they
note, a bisexual supervisor who harassed both male and
female staff members would not be making any distinction
on the basis of sex and so would be "clean" with respect to
Title VII. Here, as elsewhere, practitioners need to be certain that they can distinguish between behavior that is
clearly unjust and behavior that is illegal.

One judge cited by Ginsburg and Koreski went to great
pains to make it clear that Title VII cannot be interpreted to
include grievances involving sexual harassment. The implication? There would be too many cases for the courts to

[12] "Supreme Court Permits Firing of Gay Teacher: Refuses to Hear
Case Involving Homosexual Status, Not Conduct," *Civil Liberties*, No. 320
(November 1977), pp. 1, 7.

handle. Indeed, he said, every time a manager asked his secretary to lunch, there'd be potential for a federal case.[13]

Feminists have expressed growing discontent on the issue of harassment. One difficulty is semantic. Exactly how is harassment to be defined? It is clear that a manager who makes sexual favors a requirement for advancement or promotion is harassing employees. But what about the dirty remark? The pinch on the rear end? The half-serious invitation to bed? A community group in Ithaca, New York, conducted a "speak-out" on the subject that drew more than 100 women. These activists went into local factories and shops and interviewed 155 women (of whom some were self-selected in that they chose to come forward). No less than two-thirds reported that they had suffered sexual harassment in the workplace. Of those, 10 percent said that they had been flattered by the advances; the others felt quite the opposite. But, significantly, only a small proportion had reported the problem.

Personnel practitioners have traditionally handled the issue on a case-by-case basis, perhaps telling the man privately to cut it out and advising the woman to not let it bother her—that's just the way some men are. This may be the reason for the low reporting rate, since satisfaction is seldom granted to the grievant.

A review of the experiences of managers in handling these issues suggests only two guidelines. The first is that the presence of a staff member in personnel who is known to be sensitive to women's problems may well increase the incidence of reporting. At the same time, it may solve more of the problems in the long run, especially if they can be caught before they mushroom. The second counsel to personnel managers is that protecting the rights of grievants also protects the company. It appears that an organization can be held liable if it can be demonstrated that the organization either condoned or profited from acts of sexual

---

[13] Gilbert J. Ginsburg and Jean Galloway Koreski, "Sexual Advances by an Employee's Supervisor: A Sex-Discrimination Violation of Title VII?" *Employee Relations Law Journal*, Vol. 3 (Summer 1977), pp. 89–93.

harassment. It is, therefore, to the advantage of the personnel department not only to protect those who are being sexually harassed but to make public the company's posture toward such behavior and to keep careful records of the actions taken.

The Office Romance

A separate issue is the organizational romance. Using third-party reports, Quinn has analyzed 130 cases of men and women co-workers who became romantically involved. In 10 percent of the cases, the romance was felt to have a positive impact on the work or the workers in the department. In a third of the cases, the impact was felt to be negative but not severely so. In another third, the organizational romance was reported to have lowered morale and production and resulted in job loss.

Quinn charted management's reponses to the romances, which ranged from taking no action to offering friendly counsel to taking punitive action. Out of 130 reported intrigues, 12 women lost their jobs as opposed to 5 men.

> The female is twice as likely to be terminated as is the male. Because the male is usually in a higher position, he apparently is seen as less dispensable as the female. The female is also thought to be much less likely to benefit from an open discussion or from counseling by superiors. The latter two conditions, however, are mediated by the fact that the female's superior is often the other participant in the relationship.[14]

Although it is difficult to assess the effectiveness of intervention, it is clear that women, because of their subordinate status, are more likely to lose their jobs if they sleep where they work than men are.

The personnel practitioner is well advised to intervene

---

[14] Robert E. Quinn, "Coping with Cupid: The Formation, Impact, and Management of Romantic Relationships in Organizations," *Administrative Science Quarterly,* Vol. 22, No. 1 (March 1977), pp. 30–45, p. 44.

only if the relationship appears to be impeding the work or causing other workers to feel their rights to be infringed upon. If personnel is in the delicate position of having to "censure up"—that is, to talk with a vice president about his behavior with his secretary and to ask why she is earning three times as much as other vice presidents' secretaries—the difficulties are trebled. If it is a top management issue, personnel may well make the sound decision to let even topper management resolve it as it sees fit. But managers must, in all fairness, be certain that equal participants in any romance are punished equally. If she is transferred, he should be too. And let both of them explain that at home.

Perhaps the most ominous aspect of the office romance is that it is so often seen as inevitable. Schein has noted that fear that such relationships may develop can affect the reception accorded to women in management.[15] Sometimes managers claim that women are not placed in certain jobs because the company would get heat from men's wives if it permitted mixed-sex teams. This defense would be more credible if companies refrained from sending husbands on business trips, providing them with women secretaries, or moving executives from one part of the country to another on short notice—all because they feared the reaction of the wives. Company wives have precious little influence on company policy; it is difficult to believe that in this one area corporate gallantry prevails. It is particularly galling when the ones who suffer from such courtly decisions are women.

Increased proximity of women may cause misunderstandings to arise. Ginger-Lei Collins, driver of a semi-end dump truck on the Alaska pipeline, reports that her foreman often transferred a male driver if she had lunch with him too many times. "I went to a bar with one of the drivers one night and [the foreman] didn't speak to me for four days." [16]

---

[15] Virginia E. Schein, "Women Managers: How Different Are They?" paper presented to the American Psychological Association, Washington, D.C., September 1976.

[16] Terry Wetherby, "Up Close with Women Who Hold 'Men's Jobs,'" *New Woman*, January–February 1978, p. 41.

There is such unease about possible romantic complications among personnel at the Youngstown General Electric lamp plant that, according to a woman manager there:

> even developing simple friendships can present a challenge. Of course, there's no rule that says we have to be "good buddies" with our co-workers, but some men seem to have a more difficult time building a relationship, other than at a strictly business level, for fear that a wrong assumption might be made. It's unfortunate that mixed company at lunch, for example, is still suspect.[17]

One such suspicion resulted in personnel actions that proved to be quite expensive for management. Schoolteacher Joyce Rucker of Bowling Green, Ohio, filed a complaint under Title IX when she was demoted because of rumors that she was having an affair with a male teacher—something she denies. The male involved was promoted to an administrative job. HEW ruled it unfair to discipline only one of the teachers and has started action to cut off the more than $100,000 in federal funds going annually to the district.[18]

It is true that increased proximity of women may cause romantic relationships to develop. But having men and women as equals in a romantic intrigue may ease personnel problems substantially. The possibility of exploitation is much diminished when both participants are geologists or advertising salespeople or whatever. At least it is not automatic that one partner pays more dearly than the other.

It appears, then, that personnel can take a laissez-faire attitude. When men and women are more evenly distributed at all levels in all job sites, perhaps we can all come to experience the attraction between the sexes as something other than a terrible danger signal. No less an authority on these matters than Helen Gurley Brown, editor of *Cosmopolitan*, has written:

[17] "When the Boss Is a Woman," *For Your Information* (Public Affairs Section, General Electric), Vol. 1. No. 4 (December 1977), p. 3.

[18] "Sex Bias Cases to Cut Schools' Aid," *Ithaca (N.Y.) Journal,* March 9, 1978, p. 10.

There are no friendships between virile men and womanly women anywhere, in my opinion, completely devoid of sexual overtones. And that's good. A man always wonders what a woman is like in bed, not necessarily with him but with anybody. She wonders the same thing about him. All this speculating about men and women in offices, even if nobody does anything, causes sexy waves.[19]

Most of us will be content to let other people do the swimming and just enjoy the waves ourselves. No law against that.

[19] Helen Gurley Brown, *Sex and the Office* (New York: Pocket Books, Inc., 1965), p. 181.

> The laws of conscience, which we pretend to be derived from nature, proceed from custom.
>
> —*Montaigne, "Of Custom"*

11

What We Don't Know —and Why

IF the aim of social research is to understand human behavior—and if progress is made even fitfully toward that goal—it seems that we should be able to apply the knowledge to the solution of human problems in the workplace. To what extent can we count on social scientists to provide solid evidence that will cast light on the problems we have been focusing on here? In this chapter we will consider the limitations that current theory and methodology impose on all social research efforts and some difficulties that seem to be unique to research on women workers. We will also examine the progress that has been made in this new field and the prospects for the future.

There is a certain irony in the fact that so much of the

evidence gathered for books on women workers comes from academic life. The industry that has been the target of the most lawsuits claiming sex-based discrimination is higher education. Even as this is written, there is word that yet another institution has been charged with a Title IX violation. In the fall of 1977 a woman professor at Southern Illinois University was awarded $80,000.[1] Four women came to an out-of-court settlement with Brown University: three were awarded tenure, and the university promised to institute affirmative action measures until the underutilization of women faculty was corrected.[2] In January 1978 HEW issued word of a "major crackdown" on four more universities: Purdue, Ohio State, Michigan, and Wisconsin.[3]

Still, universities grant independence to even the most junior scholars, allowing them to speak freely and to cite evidence from specific institutions without masking sources. Indeed, faculty members at Cornell University take pride in the fact that two professors testified before the EEOC during the historic AT&T hearings. One gave evidence on behalf of management and the other on behalf of the workers. There are other reasons why studies of academic workers are used so often: costs of research at a university are attractively low; there is a captive population of young people fairly waiting to be studied; there are computers and library resources; and there is a reward structure that puts high premium on publication and wide dissemination of findings.

One price all institutions seem to pay for encouraging research is bad press. An example of this phenomenon from industry: the case of Du Pont and OSHA. Du Pont was one of the few industrial organizations to maintain safety records with sufficient accuracy to permit analysis over time, and one of the only organizations that made public its data.

[1] "Professor Wins $80,000 in Discrimination Case," *The New York Times*, September 18, 1977, p. 40.

[2] "Three Who Sued Brown University over Hiring Are Granted Tenure," *The New York Times*, September 18, 1977, p. 28.

[3] Anne C. Roark, "HEW Cracks Down on Major Universities," *Chronicle of Higher Education*, Vol. 15, No. 18 (January 16, 1978), p. 16.

Now, in discussions of OSHA enforcement, the name of Du Pont figures prominently. Thus one reason we may come to believe that universities are much more villainous than they may be is that we read about them all the time— just as we hear a great deal about the impact of various noxious substances on workers at Du Pont in part because no other organization is so upfront about its safety record.

Advantages and Limitations of the Sociological Approach

There are, it appears, at least three clear advantages to approaching a problem with the analytical tools of social science. The first is that patterns of behavior that may not have been apparent initially can be identified. Researchers can go back in history for precedent and comparison. Understanding the social forces that seem to be affecting behavior brings an almost automatic second advantage: seeing personal troubles, not as linked solely to individual weakness or venality but as due in part to outside factors. The third advantage lies in the premise that knowledge is power. To change the world, says Karl Marx, men (and women) must first understand it. To appreciate the nature of the social order is surely a prerequisite for tinkering with it, no matter how modestly.

To be sure, no sociologist is free of personal bias. According to one reviewer, Lillian Breslow Rubin's otherwise excellent social research on blue collar families is flawed by her perception of them as fatalistic about their suffering. This is due, it is said, to her background both as a clinician familiar with their problems and as a child of a working-class family for whom the pain of poverty was a daily reality. But, the reviewer notes, the author's characterization of her subjects as helpless victims is contradicted by evidence from Rubin's own life: she escaped from poverty, became a social scientist and clinician, and wrote a book.[4]

4 Barbara Laslett, review of Lillian Breslow Rubin's *Worlds of Pain: Life in the Working-Class Family* (New York: Basic Books, 1976), in *Contemporary Sociology*, Vol. 7, No. 2 (March 1978), pp. 133–136.

Before we can change American work institutions, we
must understand their organization and structure. What
tools are available for that task—or for any social science
research effort? They can be defined as follows: (1) the use
of available data, including historical evidence and current
records, (2) the method of participant observation, (3) the
survey, and (4) the laboratory experiment.

Each of the four has advantages and limitations. Historical records allow the researcher to go back and forth in time,
to study and restudy the evidence, and to test new hypotheses without fearing that the act of studying the data
changes them in any way. There are problems, however, in
that the records may not be complete or accurate, or appropriate for testing the hypotheses the researcher develops.

The method of participant observation is often criticized
as soft and subjective; it does, however, give the researcher
a firsthand feel for the human condition in a particular setting that sometimes eludes researchers using other methods
alone. The survey approach enables researchers to study
large numbers of people and develop comparisons among
them. Variations by sex, class, race, region, religion, and
nationality can be studied. But the survey has the limitation
of being only a snapshot at one point in time. The method is
weakened by the fact that only the literate respond and
perhaps only the cooperative or meek, or who knows? It is
seductive to generalize from limited responses to a large
population without explaining how it is that some answered
and some did not. Another limitation of the survey lies in
the wording of the questions. There can be wide interpretation of almost any sentence; respondents sometimes try to
expand definitions or to distort the most straightforward
concepts introduced in surveys.

The experimental method has the strong advantage of
permitting the researcher to control the study conditions
and to assess the effect of newly introduced variables.
Hypotheses can be developed in advance; the experiment
can be conducted in a laboratory or in a natural setting. But
there is always the question of generalizing from laboratory

conditions to the complexity of the real world and the seemingly inscrutable behavior of human beings in it.

These four methods and variations of them all have weaknesses; each is subject to systematic errors. One way to strengthen a research effort is to use a combination of methods so that data gathered under one method can be tested under another. If systematic analysis is abandoned altogether for wont of stronger methods, we will have to rely on polemics and ideology put forward by feminists or chauvinists and uninformed by evidence from either. That surely would not represent progress in understanding reality or narrowing the bounds of opinionated debates.

Those who seek to focus research efforts on the situation of women workers may have to cope with additional constraints. The most critical is the lack of previous work on which to build, as noted in Chapter 1. A second problem is the lack of solid theoretical analysis of the causes of inequality. No universally acceptable theories have as yet surfaced. As has been noted, explanations that rely entirely on biological or psychological factors have been found wanting, as have those that trace women's subordinate position to the political system. A third difficulty (related to the first) is the lack of available data for analysis. In an effort to remedy this problem, delegates included the following statement among the resolutions to be voted on at the National Women's Conference in Houston, Texas, in November 1977:

Resolution 24

The Office of Management and Budget should require all departments and agencies to collect, tabulate, and analyze data relating to persons on the basis of sex in order to assess the impact of their programs on women.

The U.S. Census Bureau should aggressively pursue its efforts to reduce the undercounts of minority Americans, including blacks, Hispanic Americans, Asian Americans, and American Indians. The Department of Health, Education, and Welfare should continue its ef-

forts to implement the usage of special group identifiers
in all vital-statistics recordkeeping. These statistics
should be recorded and reported by sex and subgroup.

It was passed. Researchers have at least made their dissatis-
faction known.

In times of financial stress, funding for all social research is curtailed—a problem that can be especially acute
for researchers in a new field. But even given funding, the
researchers find themselves up against new barriers. One of
these—ethical dilemmas involving privacy of records, obtaining informed consent, and so forth—is common to all
investigators. Two other barriers seem to be, if not unique
to women's studies researchers, at least especially acute for
them. They are skepticism on the part of some men and
resistance on the part of women.

The first is less of a problem today than it once was. With
the expansion of the new scholarship on women (as evidenced by the publication of journals, establishment of research institutions, and support of the ongoing research in
universities) the resistance of male researchers has diminished. Indeed, feminist men have come forward to help
the new effort; their influence has provided support when
the researchers' self-confidence flagged.

The resistance of women still poses difficulties for researchers, who are sometimes seen as having sold out.
Here, as elsewhere, an analogy to the civil rights advocates
and researchers may help. When the commitment to action
on the civil rights front rose, so did the resentment in the
black community about being studied by white researchers,
being singled out for "remedial help," and being labeled as
"disadvantaged." Psychologist Charles Thomas, writing in
the *Journal of Social Issues* in 1973, explained that "white
psychology" was not really helping to clarify the problems
because it was based on the assumption: "that black people
are similar enough to white people to permit measurement
by common instruments and different enough from white

people to justify scientific research into the causes of the differences." [5]

Even as the laws requiring employers to become more sensitive to the problems of women proliferated, some women came to resent more and more being seen as problems. A national conference on the issue of the attrition of women from engineering programs elicited testy reactions from some practicing engineers. They reiterated that they thought of themselves as engineers and not as "woman engineers" and that they would oppose any specific programs because of the implication that women were not as good as men. [6] A women's studies researcher at the University of Michigan commented bitterly that women were being "researched upon" yet once again by men. [7]

Perhaps the best (and worst) example of the conflict in priorities came about at Syracuse University, where a woman researcher set out to discover the impact on individual women of having a legal abortion, both at the time of the intervention and after the fact. She encountered some abortion referral agencies that did not, on principle, keep records, even with disguised names. A women's studies library collection was inaccessible because of the system chosen to catalog materials. Despite these difficulties, the scholarship went forward.

Old Errors Avoided in the New Studies

The "old feminists"—the suffragists who struggled against heavy odds from the 1850s to 1920 to get the vote for American women—left behind a wealth of documentation

[5] Charles W. Thomas, "The System Maintenance Role of the White Psychologist," *Journal of Social Issues*, Vol. 29, No. 1 (1973), pp. 57–65.

[6] Mary Diederich Ott and Nancy A. Reese (eds.), *Women in Engineering: Beyond Recruitment* (Ithaca, N.Y.: College of Engineering, Cornell University, 1976).

[7] Lydia Kleiner, "Research and Revolution," *University of Michigan Papers in Women's Studies*, Vol. 1, No. 3 (October 1974), pp. 185–186.

on their brave and ceaseless campaigns. Historian Eleanor
Flexner has noted that some of the chroniclers were biased
in their reporting, a limitation that made reconstruction of
the period more difficult.[8] Academic feminists in the 1970s
were on guard against that. As the decade progressed,
psychological researchers grew more careful about
generalizing from Matina Horner's pioneering work to in-
dicting all women for being fearful of success. They came to
a more sophisticated interpretation of the evidence, which
suggested that some men fear success part of the time and
some women do not fear it most of the time.[9]

While women biologists had first avoided the controversial area of sex differences perhaps because they feared the
consequences, they now moved in. Some still felt uneasy
that their findings would be used against women. Should
women prove to be more sensitive to some industrial
hazard than men, industry might use that fact to keep
women out of a whole range of skilled jobs—not just the
pertinent ones—and freeze them back at the low-skill level.

The feminist enthusiasm for the birth control pill (once
called "the great equalizer") dimmed with the growing
evidence that it had not been tested properly before it was
marketed and used daily by thousands of American women.
In the early 1970s feminists called for research on male
fertility and contraception, damning all scientists for their
willingness to experiment on women and leave men's biology alone. Now, although many still feel that research on
male contraception is long overdue, there is greater aware-
ness of how that neglect came about.

When pioneer Margaret Sanger fought for American
women's right to birth control information, it was emphasized over and over that women should not trust men to

[8] Eleanor Flexner, *Century of Struggle: The Woman's Rights Movement in the United States* (New York: Atheneum, 1974), p. 377.
[9] Phyllis Eiver, review of Mednick, Tangri, and Hoffman (eds.), *Women
and Achievement: Social and Motivational Analyses* (Washington:
Hemisphere, 1975) in *Sociology of Work and Occupations*, Vol. 4, No. 4
(November 1977), p. 480.

take precautions against unwanted conceptions. It was a woman's responsibility, the birth control advocates said, for the simple reason that she suffered more if accidents came about. Just as the Women's Bureau campaigned incessantly for protective legislation for women, so did Margaret Sanger's followers emphasize issues that were sensible at the time but that later proved to be against the interests of women in the long run.

The question of the menstrual cycle and its impact on women's capability for high-level decision making was not dismissed with a sneer as a male fantasy. Researchers and activists alike took comfort from evidence summed up by psychologist Julia Sherman:

1. Only some women are seriously affected.
2. Changes in emotions at different points in the cycle can be treated.
3. The impact of the cycle on women's performance has not been conclusively demonstrated.
4. Women appear to have cyclical differences in emotionality, but overall they are not more emotional, as a group, than men.[10]

Researchers were studying both female cycles and their counterparts in men. Among the intriguing findings: when women room together in college, their menstrual cycles come closer and closer together. More significant was the report of a female executive who had charted her own behavior over a year to find that she was indeed having more fights and finding more fault with her subordinates on days preceding the onset of her menses. Armed with that information, she was able to correct for it. And she even had the courage to share that information with others.

As research studies on biological and psychological differences between the sexes were published, fears about the wisdom of doing such work were allayed. It appeared that

[10] Julia Sherman, *On the Psychology of Women: A Survey of Empirical Studies* (Springfield, Ill.: Charles C. Thomas, 1971).

science fiction writer Isaac Asimov was almost right when he asserted in 1970 that there were only two basic differences between the sexes: "Most men are physically larger and physically stronger than most women and women get pregnant, bear babies, and suckle them. Men don't." [11]

A close analysis of the studies, both old and new, led researchers to go a bit beyond Asimov, but not much. It was agreed that girls develop faster in the preschool years than boys; that women may be, as a group, less aggressive than men; and that women may be more verbal as well, although this may be due to social expectations. Sociologists added to that short list only the evidence that in American society girls are less wanted than boys, especially as first children; that girls envy the male role from an early age more often than boys appear to envy the female role; and that, as girls grow up, they report dwindling enthusiasm for the female role.

Studies in the sociology of work based on real data and not on speculation began to appear with comforting regularity. Alice Cook devised an imaginative way to combine social research methods in studying the situation of working mothers in nine countries.[12] Good anthologies edited by Millman, Stromberg and Harkess, Glazer-Malbin, Safilios-Rothschild, and others were published, as was Barbara Wertheimer's study of working women, which rediscovered the part women have played in organized labor.

Whereas the Soviet Union's culture had been held up as more favorable to women than ours, new evidence that women physicians were in unenviable positions there accumulated. The situation of the American woman physician was analyzed in an interesting study by Kehrer, who un-

[11] Isaac Asimov, "Uncertain, Coy, and Hard to Please," in *The Solar System and Back* (Garden City, N.Y.: Doubleday, 1970).
[12] Alice H. Cook, *The Working Mother: A Survey of Problems and Programs in Nine Countries* (Ithaca, N.Y.: School of Industrial and Labor Relations, Cornell University, 1975). See also Alice H. Cook, "Working Women: European Experience and American Need," in *American Women Workers in a Full Employment Economy*, report of the Joint Economic Committee, U.S. Congress, September 15, 1977, pp. 271–306.

covered a difference in the gross income reported by physicians in 1972: men in her sample averaged $47,953 and women, $27,558. She traces possible explanations, showing that the women's specialties differ from men's, that there is a difference in average hours per week worked (for men, 51.5; for women, 41.6), and that marital status seemingly accounts for a lot of the variance in that when a male physician marries he tends to work more hours than before, while a female physician, once married, works fewer hours.[13]

Researchers were less likely to see the pay gap as due solely to discrimination against women, recognizing instead that many factors were at work. In short, closer analysis had to be done and was. Even as the psychologists reassured women by showing that the sexes are more alike than they are different, they were discovering new puzzles. The reader can find one by a simple test. Put a chair against a wall and place the toes firmly against the wall beside the chair. Step back three steps, then lean over the chair until the head touches the wall. Then try to stand up. Only people of one sex can straighten up; that fact may make some members of the other sex angry, but it does serve to demonstrate that not everything that distinguishes between women's and men's physical capabilities is understood.

The Problem of Expecting Too Much

In the late 1960s and early 1970s researchers began to have a healthy skepticism about romantic notions that change would come overnight. In 1971 Columbia's Graduate School of Business sponsored a conference entitled "Women's Challenge to Management." The proceedings were published with the coy subtitle "Corporate Lib." Edward A. Robie, senior vice president of the Equitable

---

[13] Barbara H. Kehrer, "Factors Affecting the Incomes of Men and Women Physicians: An Exploratory Analysis," *Journal of Human Resources*, Vol. 11, No. 4 (Fall 1976), pp. 526–545.

Life Assurance Company, opined that women must be welcomed into management because "industry can no longer
afford to waste so valuable a resource." Sociologist Valerie
Oppenheimer responded that she found it hard to believe
that many men would ever acknowledge that their problems were too complex for men alone to solve. Educator
Rosemary Park expressed similar skepticism: "It is by no
means evident that America needs women, or more women
than at present, to train themselves to their highest capacity
to serve the country in some way."

It would be pleasant to believe that men will actively
recruit women into high-level management jobs because
the problems are too much for mere men, but it is not a
sensible expectation. Similarly, many women became dis-
abused of the notion that government could solve the problems of half its citizens.

When President Lyndon Johnson issued the amendment to the executive order on affirmative action requiring
that women be included as a protected group, one government agency deleted sex from the amendment. So much,
one federal public servant said, for government leadership.
Others find reason for disillusionment in the fact that the
EEOC, the commission set up to administer Title VII, has
itself been the target of suits alleging sex and race discrimination.

Many feminists came to recognize that they expect too
much of women already in positions of influence. A woman
vice president remarked that she spends much more time
than she probably should on advising and counseling
younger women.[14] Kanter's analysis suggests that the lone
woman making her way in a man's world is already fighting
a "psychological cold war." [15] It seems unfair to expect her
to be nicer to protégés than men are to those lower on the
ladder. As nice, of course; nicer, no.

[14] Donald O. Jewell, "The Female Corporate Jock: What Price Equality?" *Atlanta Economic Review*, Vol. 26, No. 2 (March–April 1976), pp.
25–31.
[15] Rosabeth Moss Kanter, *Men and Women of the Corporation* (New
York: Basic Books, 1977), pp. 206–242.

In the late 1960s and early 1970s, feminists tended to believe that the very enactment of laws would solve the problems. Gilbreath, in reviewing the charges brought under Title VII as of January 1977, warned employers that "more and more women in every occupation are using it against their employers." [16] But Dunlap, analyzing the impact of Title VII, came to a different conclusion. Class relief was awarded, she noted, in only 13 percent of the sex cases and 24 percent of the race cases.[17] The existence of the law does not guarantee that it will be enforced; invoking it in a suit does not guarantee satisfaction.

In sum, many women were becoming more realistic about the nature of the problem and the length of time it would take to solve it. One pervasive belief in American life was uncovered, unlikely as it may seem, in comic strips. Researcher Gerhart Saenger analyzed 156 comic strips over time. He tabulated the personality traits of characters shown in family comics, adventure comics, and funny strips, including those about animals, and coded the interactions between characters. The most aggressive characters, he found, were single men and married women. A curious picture of American life emerged from the analysis: "Men are stronger, more powerful and vigorous than women . . . more intelligent, more logical, more predictable. The ideal married woman is more submissive and adjusts more easily."

Saenger noticed that married men were depicted as shorter, less intelligent, and more submissive and adaptable than single men. One central theme that emerges from comic strips, he concluded, is that "real men" run away from women: "Love is dangerous because it leads to marriage, a situation in which, as we have seen, men lose their strength. They can preserve their strength only by running

[16] Jerri D. Gilbreath, "Sex Discrimination and Title VII of the Civil Rights Act," *Personnel Journal*, Vol. 56, No. 1 (January 1977), pp. 23–26, p. 26.

[17] Mary C. Dunlap, "The Legal Road to Equal Employment Opportunity: A Critical View," in *American Women Workers in a Full Employment Economy*, report to the Joint Economic Committee, U.S. Congress, September 15, 1977, pp. 61–74.

away from women, who interfere with their real tasks in life, the seeking and pursuing of adventure." [18]

That gloomy picture made feminists angry; they were outraged that such a stereotype—especially one so unflattering to women as a group—should exist in the public consciousness. But now many are turning away from such preoccupations. There is no quick solution to the problem. A father can pressure a school to let his daughter compete for the tennis team, but there is no magic way for adult women to achieve the equality in the workforce they aim for.

Feminists have been criticized for alienating housewives by downgrading the importance of the homemaker role. There is irony in that statement in that the great majority of working women do their own housework as well. But it is the full-time homemaker who appears to feel threatened. Roger Morris, editor of *Context,* interviewed a number of prominent businesswomen: Katherine Graham, publisher of the *Washington Post;* Dr. Ruth Patrick, chairman of the board of directors of Du Pont; Dorothy Simon, vice president for research of Avco Corp.; Julia Walsh, vice chairman of Ferris & Co.; Esther Peterson, vice president of Giant Foods Inc.; Juliette Moran, executive vice president of GAF Corp.; Mary Head, vice chairman of the board of Amtrak; and Mary Roebling, chairman of the board of the National State Bank, Elizabeth, N.J. Among these highly visible women at the top of the corporate pyramid, there is no scorn for housewives. Indeed, Katherine Graham maintains, "The main thing has always been that women must have a choice. Some women have anxieties or feel threatened because so many other women work while they stay at home and have children. The important thing is for a woman to feel no limits on her aspirations or the kind of role she wants to live." [19]

This equating of the housewife role with the working

[18] Gerhart Saenger, "Male and Female Relations in the American Comic Strip," *Public Opinion Quarterly,* Vol. 19 (1955), pp. 195–205.
[19] Roger Morris, "Women at the Top," *Training and Development Journal,* Vol. 31, No. 5 (May 1977), pp. 39–42.

woman' role—indeed, the whole emphasis on choice—is one that many feminists reject. They deplore the housewife role, not because it isn't challenging or important but because it is dangerous. Too many housewives find themselves having to supplement their husbands' income or having to support themselves as divorcées or widows when they are not prepared to. Economist Barbara Bergmann puts it succinctly: "The housewife role is dying."[20] Many feminists have come to concur. While they recognize that it is tactless to tell a woman she hasn't chosen right when it is too late for her to change, they feel strongly that each person in this crowded world should strive for economic independence. Not emotional independence, but economic. Being trained to have "something to fall back on" in case one "fails" at marriage is not the same as having a serious full-time lifelong commitment to work.

As the Women's Bureau points out, nine out of ten girls in school today will work. So long as they are reared to believe that their life's career will be that of housewife and mother, they will be doomed to discovering too late that they must enter the workforce at a low-level job, with low reward. The realities of American life are such that relatively few men have satisfying work. Few of them feel what Graham says women should be able to feel—"no limits on the kind of role they want to live." With the rising divorce rate, more and more women will find that they have no man to support them; and they, like virtually all men, will have to work to justify the air they breathe. Few men find their way into high-level, challenging, rewarding work. But virtually *no* women do, except perhaps the few we read about in an article like Morris's. If women and men are truly to meet as equals, each must pay his or her way.

Researchers came to be humble about their ability to generalize from data on middle-class people.[21] Where there

[20] Barbara Bergmann, quoted in "Housewifery Has No Good Future," *Cornell Chronicle*, Vol. 8, No. 27 (April 21, 1977), pp. 3, 6.
[21] Sally Hillsman Baker, "Women in Blue Collar and Service Occupations," in Ann H. Stromberg and Shirley Harkess (eds.), *Women Working: Theories and Facts in Perspective* (Palo Alto, Cal.: Mayfield, 1978), pp. 339–376.

once had been acceptance of the somewhat arrogant notion that middle-class families were more "liberated" from rigid sex role expectations than benighted blue collar families, now there was uncertainty. The Davidsons challenged the accepted view with solid evidence. They made 21 comparisons between classes (measured by occupation) and found statistically significant differences in only three—and in one of those cases the blue collar group proved to be more egalitarian.[22]

Researchers began to be leery about defining a "feminine" style as opposed to a "masculine" one and to eschew entirely any predictions about how humane the world would be if women instead of men were running big corporations or political parties.[23] In fact, as the new scholarship came of age, researchers began to realize just how little they knew and how many big questions remained.

The Most Challenging Questions

The research suggests that parents and society in general have made too much of the differences between the sexes. Suppose that differentiation were eliminated entirely and children were not told which sex they were until it became obvious at puberty. A story in *Ms* magazine told about a child known as "X" who was never told its sex. "X" was dressed in overalls in grade school; the other children were bewildered when "X" proved to be as good at football as at sewing; "X" didn't seem to mind not knowing which sex it was.

One implication of that fictional account is that parents cannot do it alone. As psychologist John Condry points out, children are subject to powerful influences outside the family. If a daughter spends a third of her waking hours at home

[22] Chandler Davidson and Virginia M. T. Davidson, "Variations in Gender-Role Equality Among Classes: A Research Note," *Sex Roles*, Vol. 3, No. 5 (1977), pp. 459–467.

[23] Patricia J. Marcum, "Men *and* Women on the Management Team," *University of Michigan Business Review*, Vol. 28, No. 4 (November 1976), pp. 8–11.

or in the neighborhood, an additional third in school, and the other third watching television, then she receives many more messages about what it means to be female than the signals her parents transmit to her. Feminist Condry points out that it is no wonder that so little is understood about the acquisition of gender role and the extent to which this can be separated from developing sexuality: the school as it is known today is a century old; television as a socializing medium, perhaps 25 years old.[24]

Speaking as a parent, Condry is leery of advocating that parents use their own children as battering rams against established social norms. But parents are trying to change the way they rear their children, as can be seen from a father's account of the real-life reactions of 16-year-old boys to the fact that his daughter is good at football.[25]

The immediate question of interest to parents is how the educational system can be changed to give girls an equal chance with boys for full physical and intellectual development. Research at a coeducational university has suggested that that setting has clear drawbacks for college women.[26] Jill Conway, president of Smith College, cites the opinion of a New College don at Oxford University in 1963 to the same effect:

"In general, young men are best educated in the company of young women. Young women are best educated in the company of their own sex. These two principles are hard to reconcile." [27]

While academicians try to reconcile principles, personnel practitioners and policy makers in industry get precious little help in determining how they can best provide programs to reeducate women and men reared in the old way.

[24] John Condry, "The Acquisition of Gender Roles and the Concept of Control," presentation made to the Graduate Faculty, Women's Studies, Cornell University, Ithaca, N.Y., March 16, 1978.

[25] Charles Tekeyan, "When the Football Star's a Girl," *The New York Times,* March 19, 1978, Section 5, p. 2.

[26] Jennie Farley, "Coeducation and College Women," *Cornell Journal of Social Relations,* Vol. 9, No. 1 (Spring 1974), pp. 87–97.

[27] Jill Conway, "Viewpoint: Women's Place," *Change Magazine,* March 1978, pp. 8–9.

Social research on the nature of women and men is in its infancy; sociology is today where chemistry was when it was alchemy. Researchers cannot yet be counted on to provide the kind of solid data to corporate policy makers that will insure the success of affirmative action programs. But researchers can at least provide evidence that, for all its limitations, tells us something important.

It can be said with confidence that Freud was mistaken when he attributed all women's psychological problems to "penis envy." We can also disregard the facile generalizations surfacing in popular books to the effect that women would be successful in business if they only dressed for the job. Management consultant Betty Harragan may well be right in advising women to wear tailored suits at work rather than flowered dresses. She notes, for example, that it is convenient to work in shirtsleeves and then, when going to a meeting, to put on a jacket that has both the advantage of having pockets to put things in and the symbolic value of putting on the "mantle of power." But we cannot say women have "pockets envy."

Linguists may be right when they suggest that the way we talk about things both reflects and affects the way we think about them. When feminists at the Harvard Divinity School began to agitate for change in interpretations of scripture so that the deity could be addressed as she (or at least be thought to have "feminine" as well as "masculine" qualities), linguists at Harvard dismissed the issue as a manifestation of "pronoun envy." Every businessman who interrupts himself in the course of a speech to change "he" to "he or she" in deference to women's sensibilities knows that language is important—but it isn't everything.

Perhaps the best counsel we can give social researchers is that they try to have a little "practitioner envy"—to undertake studies that will permit policy makers to make hard decisions based on evidence of what programs truly work. If researchers and practitioners worked more closely on the problems of integrating women into all levels of the workforce, there might be, at the very least, less reliance on the courts as the final arbiter of how to solve problems.

To determine whether you are being fair to the businesswomen in your life, ask yourself . . .

Am I trying to protect someone who needs no protection?
Do I take her as seriously as her contribution warrants? . . .

Above all, ask: Would I treat a man the same way?

—*Richard R. Saltzmann,*
"Working with Women" [1]

12

What We Do Know

FEMINISTS—activists and researchers alike—appear to be moving away from simplistic explanations of events as they are. Few believe that women are helpless pawns in a system they never made, just as few accept the notion that women are crippled by psychological or biological weaknesses. Life would be easier if causes were so readily identified. If the "pawn" theory were supported by evidence, all

[1] Richard R. Saltzmann, "Working with Women: How & Where & Why & When—Plus Five Ways to Bumble, " *Marketing Times*, Vol. 24, No. 2 (March–April 1977), pp. 12–15.

we would have to do is change the political system and liberation would follow as the night the day. But evidence from controlled economies suggests otherwise. If women's fear of success were the only culprit, women would be fine if they'd just pull up their socks. But we know that all the assertiveness in the world cannot provide jobs where there are none. If biology is the villain at base, then women should accept the news and go back home to expend their energies on being "total women." Which, of course, many cannot do.

The easy answers do not appear to be adequate. We have seen that the problem of women's second-class status remains. This is not a new issue. The Bible sets forth in no uncertain terms the value of human beings (Leviticus 27:3–7). Infants are valued differentially: for a boy of one month to five years, 5 shekels; for his twin sister, 3 shekels. Between the ages of five and twenty years, the male is valued at 20 shekels, the female at 10. From twenty to sixty: the male, 50 and the female, 30. And for those over sixty years of age: the man, 15 shekels; the woman, 10 shekels.

Some young people today appear to believe that the problems have been resolved. They have not. Despite breathless reports in the mass media about the new egalitarian marriages, researchers have concluded that husbands and wives are seldom equal partners. The Rapoports studied couples in England; [2] Ginsburg analyzed a group of highly educated women on the East Coast; [3] Poloma looked at professional pairs on the West Coast.[4] Almost always and everywhere, it seems, wives accept the premise that their husbands' jobs come first and that housework and child care are her responsibility. Economist Kathryn Walker has demonstrated that the working wife gets little assistance from either her husband or her children even when she spends

[2] Robert Rapoport and Rhona Rapoport, *Dual-Career Families* (New York: Penguin Books, 1971).

[3] Eli Ginsburg and Alice M. Yohalem, *Educated American Women: Self-Portraits* (New York: Columbia University Press, 1966).

[4] Margaret M. Poloma, "The Myth of the Egalitarian Family: Familial Roles and the Professionally Employed Wife," paper presented at the American Sociological Association annual meeting, 1970.

as many hours at her paying job as her husband does at his.[5] Indeed, when the wife goes to work, one unexpected consequence is additional free time for the husband.[6] The International Labor Organization had called attention to the worldwide phenomenon of the doubly burdened working mother. Yet the fact remains that, according to one study as least, the mental health of the working-wife/mother is, if not as good as that of her husband, certainly better than that of the housewife/mother.[7] One effect of being married is that the measured IQ appears to go down, and, as has been noted, participation in political activity declines with the birth of a child.

But the most devastating consequence of being female appears to come about in the workplace. The assumptions about the nature of masculinity and the nature of femininity apparently impede many managers from giving full and fair consideration to women candidates for employment, promotion, and training. The government is attempting to solve these problems by regulating behavior at work.

Other forms of injustice have only begun to come to light and are less amenable to legal solution. One is that women age faster socially (and with more devastating consequences) than men do. By that is meant that, when fraternal twins are middle-aged, the man is somehow seen as younger than his sister. A second: it seems clear that a wider range of physical attractiveness is acceptable for men than for women. The excessive attention paid to the way women look appears to cripple the occupational chances of many. Journalist Gael Greene has termed it "pretty-face privilege": the fact that women who are judged beautiful by current standards have unfair advantages. It may always be the case that men who are tall and deemed attractive have

[5] Kathryn Walker and Margaret Woods, *Time Use: A Measure of Household Production of Family Goods and Services* (Washington, D.C.: American Home Economics Association, 1976).

[6] John P. Robinson et al., "Sex Role Differences in Time Use," *Sex Roles*, Vol. 3, No. 5 (October 1977), pp. 443–458, p. 451

[7] Walter R. Gove and Michael R. Geerken, "The Effect of Children and Employment on the Mental Health of Married Men and Women," *Social Forces*, Vol. 56, No. 1 (September 1977), pp. 56–66.

an extra edge granted by luck. So it may be with women. The unfairness comes about because appearance is so much more important for women that ordinary-looking women are disadvantaged in comparison with ordinary-looking men. Sociologist Constantina Safilios-Rothschild had predicted optimistically that this will change.[8] As women become more economically independent, the way they look will be less important, as will their age.

A sidelight on the nature of stereotypes gives heartening evidence here. When women are few at a coeducational institution, an "ugly coed" myth develops. Men speak of the women with scorn as having fat legs, being funny-looking, stuck-up, and obnoxious. As the number of women increases, the myth dies away. Similarly, when a few men are admitted to a formerly all-female college, they are deemed to be "jerks," "creeps," "dopes," and in fact often labeled as gays. But these myths fade as the numbers balance out. So it may be in the work world as more women enter male fields, whereas the careerwoman of today is thought by many to be a tough babe with jangling bracelets and a bitchy temperament, in the future women may come to be recognized to be as various and as individual as the men they work with.

A major problem often cited by feminists is the lack of role models. How can women be expected to aspire to occupations that are not traditional for their sex—or indeed to form realistic ideas about the likelihood of working at all—when the working woman is still invisible in American life? Where are the American heroines, the ones who could inspire young girls to achievement in science, business, political life? They are few and far between. As has been noted, the history of women's contribution to American life had been largely lost. Only now are historians uncovering their story.

---

[8] Constantina Safilios-Rothschild, "Women and Work: Policy Implications and Prospects for the Future," in Stromberg and Harkess (eds.), *Women Working: Theories and Facts in Perspective* (Palo Alto, Cal.: Mayfield, 1977) pp. 419–433.

One indication of the invisibility of women in the national consciousness is the extent to which women have been honored on postage stamps. Hundreds of stamps have pictured individual men as presidents, poets, statesmen, business leaders, inventors, military leaders. But women have been honored only 51 times. Of these, 22 stamps have been issued to salute women as a group—as mothers, teachers, nurses, social workers. Individual American heroines have been honored on postage stamps only 29 times. A countertrend can be seen in the series of sugar packages put out by International Automated Machines, Inc., in Perrysburg, Ohio. There we see pictures of (and biographies of) women of accomplishment. The absence of women's faces from postage stamps, the recognition of American women on sugar packages, pressure for changes in the way we address and refer to women—these and similar issues are often dismissed as trivia. They must be understood in a larger context, however, for the light they cast on the major problems.

The important issues, from the point of view of women workers, have only begun to be addressed. While managers change their policies in recruitment, selection, and training, other major problems remain to be resolved. The provision of maternity benefits, of equal pensions, of equal benefits from the social security system, and of benefits for part-time workers are goals not yet reached. Similarly, the lack of corporate willingness to experiment with flextime jobs and jobs that can be shared by two people is bemoaned. There is the problem of child care—ever present and difficult.

For the present, the major difficulty seems to be the nature of the work women do. That half the human race should be disproportionately represented in routine low-paying occupations is an injustice that cannot be ignored. Nor can it be changed overnight. The very way jobs are structured—narrowing the tasks as much as possible to shorten training time—results in women doing jobs, as one researcher has noted, that can be done by pigeons. He points out that a drug company experimented with training birds to separate pills into piles, the very task many women do. The pigeons could do the work faster and with fewer errors than the people. As it developed, the idea never went beyond the experimental stage. Problems of hygiene intervened. Pigeons aren't as clean as women, nor can they be instructed to wash their hands. It has also been suggested that the job of bank teller is well suited to people with mental handicaps. A retarded person could be working at the top of his or her ability paying and receiving. Ninety percent of bank tellers are women. Of these, many are wasting gifts that could be used fruitfully, if we only had the imagination to figure out how.

Analysis of the occupational outlook for many of the jobs currently done by women does not augur well for the future. Ginsburg has predicted that the nature of work available to women will decline rather than improve in quality.[9] Baker, writing about blue collar women and the future of their jobs, speculates that the paucity of opportunities will bring about a more inequitable distribution of wealth in the United States than exists now.[10] Blue collar women marry blue collar men; the gap in income and opportunities between working-class families and middle-class families will widen. A report to the Joint Economic Committee of Congress shows that women workers are particularly vulnerable to downswings in the economy. The economic status of women workers, then, worsens at the very time when they and their children need increased income.[11]

Personnel practitioners may well feel that resolution of the problems between the sexes should not be laid on them. Indeed, it should not. Despite the uneven division of labor

[9] Eli Ginsburg, "The Job Problem," *Scientific American*, Vol. 237, No. 5 (November 1977), p. 43.
[10] Sally Hillsman Baker, "Women in Blue Collar and Service Occupations," in Stromberg and Harkess (eds.), *Women Working*, p. 371.
[11] "The Impact of Macroeconomic Conditions on Employment Opportunities for Women," study prepared for the Joint Economic Committee, U.S. Congress, January 1977.

between men and women in the home, the government has not yet entered the kitchen to legislate who does what. Similarly, it cannot be expected that appreciation of good-looking people of either sex will be outlawed. Nor can personnel practitioners have a direct impact on the long-range job outlook of the specialties for which women or men are trained.

Still, personnel managers may have found that the social and economic realities of women's disadvantaged status came home to them as parents or spouses long before any new feminist movement or any government regulations were on the scene. Perhaps the manager or a close relative was the first woman in a formerly male job; she knows the intense pressure and loneliness that accompany the satisfaction of finding women can do men's work and earn men's pay. The manager may know firsthand that working couples are severely penalized by the current income tax system for being married rather than living together. Or the manager may have been involved firsthand in the endless debate over seniority versus affirmative action that so divides women and minority men from the unions, which could be their allies.

Personnel managers who know these problems well can deal more sympathetically with women workers with grievances. As Pendergrass notes, the effective counselor of women with sex discrimination complaints doesn't expect to hear low-key "ladylike" presentations of problems; the grievants have very likely tried everything "nice" they could think of before they got to personnel.[12] The effective manager knows that most women do not even recognize that they *are* being discriminated against. Researchers found a $3,500 difference in male/female income due to discrimination (defined here as nonachieved advantage); "95 percent of the women in their sample had lower

[12] Virginia Pendergrass et al., "Sex Discrimination Counseling," *American Psychologist,* Vol. 31, No. 1 (January 1976), pp. 36–45.

salaries than men in equivalent positions, but only 7.9 percent of the women said they thought they had been discriminated against." [13]

Management consultants Margaret Hennig and Anne Jardim recount the reaction of a businessman who had not considered the implications of today's economic realities for his own daughter:

> In our professional work, we have often spent many hours convincing a man in management that it was important for him to try to understand the differences which women were bringing to the organizational setting. He would respond to our argument by repeating again and again that he agreed that men and women are different but that he thanked God that they are. He would agree that women are less successful in management careers but say thank God that is so. . . . [Finally] we would say to him . . . "If you had known on the day your daughter was born that starting at the age of twenty she would have to work continuously to survive, would you have done anything differently with her than you have done up until now?" . . . One corporate senior vice-president . . . said, "I feel sick to my stomach. If she has to work, then I have done it all wrong." [14]

Whether managers choose to change their style as parents is not (thank goodness) a matter for the government to decide. Their style as managers, however, is, as Hennig and Jardim note. The question is not *if* but *how*—either voluntarily or by imposed solution. Managers can go the route of the John Hancock Mutual Life Insurance Co. and fight the

[13] Teresa Levitin et al., "Sex Discrimination Against the American Working Woman," cited in Robert N. Stern et al., "Equality for Blacks and Women: An Essay on Relative Progress," *Social Science Quarterly*, Vol. 56, No. 4 (March 1976), pp. 664–662.
[14] Margaret Hennig and Anne Jardim, *The Managerial Woman* (Garden City, N.Y.: Doubleday/Anchor, 1977), pp. 203–204.

government at every step as company policy.[15] Or as individuals they can get into shouting matches with representatives of women's organizations who come with television cameras at the ready, as happened at the Harris Trust & Savings Bank in Chicago.[16] Or they can try to be prepared to avert that kind of trouble.

Responsible feminists today are slow to urge women workers to sue. Experience has shown that it is a long, agonizing process, as expensive in time and emotion as it is in money. Women who sue become almost consumed with their grievances. But when their cause is just, when they are already resentful because of the treatment they have had, a suit seems to be the only route open. Managers may be able to forestall those draining legal actions by making truly good-faith efforts to provide equal opportunity in the workplace. It is hard to believe that any worker relishes the thought of lengthy court proceedings or that any manager welcomes the chance to give up the right to make important managerial decisions.

Can there be a meeting ground between a feminist and a staunch defender of tradition? A women's movement leader shocked the medical community in 1968 with a fiery speech:

> Women have been *murdered* by their so-called *function* of childbearing exactly as black people were murdered by their *function* of *color*. . . . The function of childbearing is the function of men oppressing women. Marriage and family are as corrupt institutions as slavery ever was. . . .
>
> It's irrelevant to the emancipation of women what happens when women free themselves from the institutions that maintain them in their oppressed state. It wasn't the responsibility of the slaves to think up, develop, ex-

[15] Liz Roman Gallese, "Battle over Bias: Some Companies Fight Tougher Federal Drive on Job Discrimination," *The Wall Street Journal*, February 17, 1978, p. 1.

[16] Joann S. Lublin, "Secretaries' Revolt: Female Office Workers Form Groups to Fight Sex Bias, Petty Chores," *Wall Street Journal*, February 24, 1978, p. 1.

periment, and prove superior a new economic system for the South before they were emancipated, and it's not our job to figure out what happens to the kiddies before women free themselves. . . .[17]

In contrast, there is the conservative columnist and television interviewer who believes that permitting women to enter fields traditionally restricted to men spells the end of civilized life:

If a republic permits, nay encourages, women to take up any profession, particularly such a profession as encourages the cultivation of aggressiveness, the killer instinct, ruthlessness, we are abandoning those forms—order and fashion—that have defended the venerable distinctions. [The result will be] . . . the masculinization of women . . . [and the abandoning of "vital brakes" for men] against sheer licentiousness of conduct.[18]

The problem of trying to reconcile these two extremes will not go away. As Susan B. Anthony said, there will never be "another season of silence until women have the same rights men have on this green earth." Nor will the effort to find the middle ground result in anarchy being loosed upon the world. Good women and good men will build a strong, well-founded center, respecting one another's rights and bearing mutual responsibility for children, whose welfare is never irrelevant to anything. And, as America moves into its third century, that strong center will hold.

[17] Ti-Grace Atkinson, speech delivered to the Medical Committee for Human Rights, Philadelphia, Pa., April 5, 1968, mimeographed. (Emphasis is Atkinson's.)

[18] William F. Buckley, "Ladies in the Foxholes?" Syndicated column (*Syracuse Post Standard*, March 17, 1978, p. 5).

Index

abolitionists, 102–103
absences from work
  child-related, 171–172
  by women, 28–29
Acker, Joan, 3
address, forms of, 150–153
administrative jobs, 8
advertisements
  spurious, 50, 53
  wording of, 46, 42
affectional preference, *see*
  homosexuality
affirmative action
  false company claims of, 109
  impact of, 14–17
  personnel departments' responsibilities for, 23–25
*Affirmative Action and Equal
  Employment: A Guidebook
  for Employers* (EEOC),
  23*n*., 36*n*., 39*n*., 57*n*.
affirmative action plans
  managers' sabotage of, 162
  required of federal contractors by Executive Order,
  13

AFL-CIO, 127, 128
age
  discrimination by, 40, 175
  see also older women
Age Discrimination in Employment Act of 1967
  (U.S.), 12
aggressiveness, seen as negative trait in women, 83
Almquist, Elizabeth M., 169
Alpander, Guvenc G., 78–79,
  85*n*.
American Association of University Women, 151
American Broadcasting Company, 124–125
American Council on Education, 96
American Telephone & Telegraph Company (AT&T)
  cash judgments against, 123
  discrimination hearings on,
  184
  internal hiring in, 47
  men entering "women's
  jobs" in, 69

Sixty Words Per Minute, 129
Smith, Margaret Chase, 115
Smith, Robert S., 14*n.*, 110
smoking clinics, 89–90
social classes, generalizing
across, 197–198
social work, 143
sociological research, 185–189,
192–194, 200
Southern Illinois University,
184
Soviet Union, 192
Spain, Jayne B., 117*n.*, 118*n.*
Spinner, Francis Elias, 117–118
spouses
interview questions about, 45
see also marriage
Spradley, James, 138
Spriestersbach, D. C., 15*n.*
Staines, Graham, 144*n.*
Standard Oil of New Jersey,
123
Stanton, Elizabeth Cady, 102,
103, 106
states
antidiscrimination legislation
in, 14
women employed by, 121–
122
*Statistical Abstract of the
United States* (1976), 97*n.*
statistics, misstatements of,
109–110
Steinberg, Diane B., 121–122
Stephens, John L., 129–130
Stern, Harry, 88–89
Stern, Robert N., 143*n.*
stewardesses, 175
Strainchamps, Ethel, 49*n.*
Stromberg, Ann H., 192
Strong Vocational Interest Test,
69–70
success, fear of, 144–146, 190,
202
suffragists, 102–103, 189–190

supervisors
affirmative action plans sabo-
taged by, 162
attitudes of, 208–209
employee evaluations by,
47
men's resentment of women
as, 30–31
recruitment preferences of,
43–44
training recommendations
by, 80
survey research, 186
Survey Research Center, 160
Sweden
problems of women entering
traditionally male trades in,
84
quotas in, 58–59
Syme, G. J., 34*n.*
Syracuse University, 189
systematic discrimination,
64–71
veterans preference, as form
of, 122
systematic error, in research,
187

teaching, 143
Tekeyan, Charles, 199*n.*
television
discrimination actions in,
124–125
women portrayed on, 25
Tepperman, Jean, 141
Terborg, James R., 60–61, 144
testing
for internal hiring, 47–48
systematic discrimination in,
69–70
testees' reactions to, 60
theology, 200
Thomas, Charles, 188–189
Tidball, M. Elizabeth, 68*n.*
Tiger, Lionel, 31

women's colleges, recruitment at, 44, 45
women's liberation movement
black women and, 102–108
increase of women in workforce and, 6, 10
see also feminists
Women Workers Today (U.S. Dept. of Labor), 7, 8
Woodcock, Leonard, 114
Woods, Margaret, 203*n.*
word-of-mouth job announcements, 37, 38, 41–42
word processing, 141
work
definitions of, 133–135
romances at, 179–182
sexual harassment at, 177–179
social customs in, 153–159
time and effort put into, 160

workforce
black women in, 97–98
occupational groups in, 8
proportion of women in, from 1952 to 1977, 6
women's commitment to, 28
women's participation in, by age, 168–169
Working Women Organizing Project, 129
World Antislavery Convention (1840), 102
World War II
child care during, 169–170
guidelines on supervision of women workers, 4–5
Wyatt, Addie, 135
Wyoming, 149–150

yearbook photos, study of, 32
Yohalem, Alice M., 202*n.*